ENCYCLOPEDIA Gothica

ENCYCLOPEDIA
Gothica

LIISA LADOUCEUR

Illustrations by **GARY PULLIN**

ECW Press

Published by ECW Press
2120 Queen Street East, Suite 200, Toronto, Ontario, Canada M4E 1E2
416-694-3348/info@ecwpress.com

LIBRARY AND ARCHIVES CANADA CATALOGUING IN PUBLICATION

Ladouceur, Liisa
Encyclopedia Gothica / Liisa Ladouceur.

ISBN 978-1-77041-024-4
ALSO ISSUED AS: 978-1-77090-080-6 (PDF); 978-1-77090-079-0 (EPUB)

1. Goth culture (Subculture)—Encyclopedias. 1. Title.

HM646.L33 2011   306'.103   C2011-902859-X

Editors: Michael Holmes and Crissy Boylan
Cover and interior illustrations: Gary Pullin
Text design: Tania Craan
Typesetting: Gail Nina
Production: Troy Cunningham
Printing: Courier   1   2   3   4   5

The publication of Encyclopedia Gothica has been generously supported by the Canada
Council for the Arts which last year invested $20.1 million in writing and publishing
throughout Canada, and by the Ontario Arts Council, an agency of the Government
of Ontario. We also acknowledge the financial support of the Government of Canada
through the Canada Book Fund for our publishing activities, and the contribution
of the Government of Ontario through the Ontario Book Publishing Tax Credit.
The marketing of this book was made possible with the support of the Ontario Media
Development Corporation.

Canada Council   Conseil des Arts
for the Arts   du Canada

Canada

ONTARIO ARTS COUNCIL
CONSEIL DES ARTS DE L'ONTARIO

PRINTED AND BOUND IN THE UNITED STATES

"Black.
Black planet.
Black.
Black world."

— The Sisters of Mercy

This book is dedicated to all the children of the night.

In your darkness, you make the world a more colourful place.

You are, like beauty and poetry, immortal.

TABLE OF CONTENTS

INTRODUCTION

What Is "What Is Goth"?

Ask a Goth person "What is Goth?" and they'll likely tell you, "I'm not Goth." Which is a sure sign that they are, in fact, %666 Goth. If you find this confusing, this book is for you. If this makes perfect sense, this book is for you — but it is also about you.

It's no wonder that the G-word perplexes both insiders and on-lookers alike. This one hard-working four-letter word has been asked to define so many things: music, fashion, architecture, typefaces, literature, cinema, a Germanic tribal horde and, for about 30 years now, the kind of people prone to hanging out in graveyards sipping red wine and pretending it's blood while reading Shelley aloud and contemplating the bleakness of existence (and/or holing up in their bedrooms with Joy Division records). At least that's who one might think a Goth person is by the way we are most often portrayed in news reports and the kind of articles that pop up around Halloween or whenever a teenager wearing a black T-shirt shoots someone.

I say "we" here because I am, unabashedly, Goth.

I wasn't born that way, a daughter of darkness. But it didn't take much. In fact it took exactly 4 minutes and 20 seconds of television. MuchMusic, then the Nation's Music Station in Canada, had just come to my area and, being obsessed with popular music, I watched every day after school. And on one afternoon in the late 1980s Much played "She Sells Sanctuary" by a British band I didn't know, The Cult. Like most videos of the era, it was a simple performance clip, the band lip-synching and fake-playing in a studio — in this case one bathed in psychedelic coloured lights. It's not, viewed today, particularly Goth. (Singer Ian Astbury is dressed like a hippie and guitarist Billy Duffy has short white blond hair, to start.) But its opening moments — a red curtain parts to reveal a shadowy, Shaman-type figure all in black slowly swirling his hands around in a fog — hypnotized me like nothing I'd seen before. And the song itself — with its incessant drumbeat, intoxicating echoey guitar riffs and infectiously simple, haunting refrain about the world dragging us down was my first exposure to something that bombastically melodramatic. I knew melancholy from poetry, but this was ache you could dance to. For me, being exposed to "She Sells Sanctuary" was like getting a blood transfusion: I woke up afterwards and my insides were completely different. I had a totally new pulse.

After The Cult came The Cure. And Love and Rockets and Bauhaus and The Sisters of Mercy and

Siouxsie and everything else I could get my hands on in a small town, pre-internet. A random photo of three scary looking guys in a free magazine turned me on to Skinny Puppy, and from them came the discovery of industrial music. By this point, I had moved to Toronto, knew the word "Goth," and was well on my way to exploring everything that meant. Ultimately, I started publishing my own fanzine (*The Ninth Wave*, named after an album side by Kate Bush) and guest co-hosting a campus radio show, Beyond the Gates of Hell, with the Gothiest boy in town. It was about this time that I started being asked, "What is Goth?" A lot. Especially by the media.

On many occasions I primped for evening news cameras or wayward reporters and tried my best to explain what the hell all this was. I would declare how we are not (all) suicidal or satanic, speak haughtily of a love for poetry and philosophy and beauty and romance, trying my best to convey, in a way that just might make it into the inevitably truncated sound-bite, just what is Goth.

I was, of course, doomed.

Since it first crawled out of the clubs of England and America in the death throes of the 1970s, the subculture we've come to call Goth has been difficult to explain. At the start, these denizens of the night were known as batcavers or death rockers, the music was generally considered part of post-punk and the clothes were simply . . . black. Mystery lingers over who first appropriated the word "Goth" to describe this new kind of young freak; my beloved Ian Astbury (one of those Goth icons who insists he's not Goth at all) is just one who has staked his claim to it.

By the mid-1980s, the G-word was well established, and a collective consciousness evolved around the term. Gothic rock was a legit musical genre. There were Goth-specific shops, Goth magazines and Goth festivals. Goth was now a somewhat recognizable thing, a world of Victorian- or Medieval-inspired sense and sensibilities co-mingling with punk rock and S&M attitude and fashion. And the diverse crew of anarchists, art school brats and horror movie fans who had started it seemed to have been distilled into a fairly homogenous bunch — one quite easy to identify. Or so we thought. Thanks to explosion of the internet in the mid-1990s these people — many of them misfits in small towns around the globe — started to find each other in great numbers. And as they chatted amongst themselves, they discovered that as much as they were all drawn to what had come to be known as Goth, they weren't necessarily alike. A popular question became, "Is [this thing I like/hate] Goth?" Because, like any good species seeking immortality, the subculture was mutating, drawing upon new influences such as cyberpunk, rave culture and anime and finding new ways of expressing a devotion to the dark side beyond black eyeliner and backcombed hair. The different factions named themselves: rivetheads, Cybergoths, Romantigoths, etc. Each new wave brought their own codes of conduct and methods of communication. For the one thing these sub-groups had in common was that each sought to distinguish itself from the others, and from youth culture trends at large. And so, Goths reevaluated what the G-word meant, twisting it into new variations to suit the bewildering number of subgenres and sub-subgenres, so much so that terms such as Trad Goth emerged to distinguish the old-school original folk from the new.

The net.goths also developed their own particular parlance, a mash-up of in-jokes and slang designed mostly for self-amusement but also serving to keep outsiders out, or at least make fun of them when they crept 'round. ("Them" meaning mostly the legions of spooky kids adopting Goth in the late 1990s in wake of the mainstream popularity of Hot Topic and Marilyn Manson.) If you've ever thought Goths take themselves too seriously, you've never watched them make up names for their silly dance moves or craft Goth specific pick-up lines. (You can look up Pulling the Taffy and Nice Boots in the pages that follow.) Valiant attempts to catalogue this Goth talk were made, with FAQs helping Babybats and Elder Goths alike decipher an ever-evolving lexicon of musical genres, clothing styles, communities, and so on. But as the web grew, these resources fell fallow. Now, as a second and third generation of children of the night have come into their own, with their own bands, fashion and texting or IM shorthands, it seems we're barely speaking the same language anymore.

So it's no real surprise that it's more difficult than ever to actually explain What Is Goth. You could turn to the *Oxford English Dictionary*, but even it has trouble:

> Goth: 1. a member of a Germanic people that invaded the Roman Empire in the third and fifth centuries. 2. an uncivilized or ignorant person. 3. (goth) a) a style of rock music derived from punk, often with apocalyptic or mystical lyrics. b) member of a subculture favouring black clothing, black and white make-up, metal jewelry and goth music.

As a self-professed word geek I am loath to pick a fight with the mighty OED. Yet as a Goth Girl, I must. For while I am certain that those who laboured over this particular entry were as scrupulous as can be, in their brevity they have failed to suitably put to rest the question of What Is Goth? Rather, in boiling it down to three parts fashion to one part music (which wouldn't be quite so insulting if they didn't list black-clad youths and our "apocalyptic" racket after an archaic definition of Goth as an "uncivilized or ignorant person") they have reminded us that the guardians of language have not kept up with all the ways in which this word has evolved, its myriad meanings.

What about the academics, then? Yes, they too have tackled the question. In the past decade, several dense explorations of our spooky sub-cultural capital have emerged to line university library shelves — essays and treatises on Goth identity by curious English professors and music critics and sociologists and historians. If you devour these works you may come out armed with more highfalutin words to describe our bonds (and our bondage attire) but not a useful definition of What Is Goth.

In defense of hardworking dictionary editors, reporters and scholars everywhere, this is, after all, an unpopular culture. It not only lurks in shadows, it lingers, it loves, it *lives* to be mysterious. Despite this, the first rule of Fright Club has never been "Don't talk about Fright Club." In fact, quite the opposite. Goths spend an extraordinary amount of time discussing and debating and defining their Gothness. The way Goths talk about being Goth (or not Goth) is as intrinsic to the culture as big boots and a copy of The Cure's *Disintegration*. It is precisely our distinct lexicon (and the black humour that goes with it) that most distinguishes us from the similarly pale-faced, apocalypse-obsessed Norwegian black metal church burners, emo wristcutters and anyone else wandering back alleys in cloaks after dark. If you truly want to understand us, you need to participate in the ongoing dialogue about What Is Goth. So why hasn't all this (pierced) navel-gazing translated to the world at large?

It's fair to say that Goths aren't too keen to talk to outsiders about this lifestyle. Perhaps because the conversations so often begin with "Why do you wear black?" — a question to which most of us truly have no answer. Or perhaps because no matter what we say in interviews the media always spits out the same shallow stereotype. For every bang-on interpretation (*Saturday Night Live*'s "Goth Talk" or the Goth Kids of *South Park*), there are many more network crime dramas or daytime talk shows that get it completely wrong — all blood drinking and Satanic Bible toting. Granted, it's hard to blame them. If we can't even define ourselves, how is a TV writer (who probably works in a state where it's sunny all the time) supposed to get it right?

Once upon a time, being misunderstood was not actually a big deal. It made us laugh, a somewhat welcome affirmation of our outsider status. Then came the Columbine massacre in 1999, wrongly attributed to teenage Goths, and a shitstorm of panic rained down on trench coat–clad kids everywhere, especially in Middle America. Suddenly, the fact that the public at large had no clue what Goth was became a pretty big problem for a lot of people. Goths had joined the ranks of heavy metal music fans as alleged devil worshipping threats to The Children. We were victims of ignorance heightened by hysterical media stories and gossip.

And that is one reason I wanted to write this book. Beyond my word nerdiness and my passion for documenting subculture, I wanted to do my best to counter the notion that Goth is about violence, about self-harm, about depression or destruction or evil. I knew that it was about music and fashion and art and history and the appreciation of nature. (Well, at least bats.)

And I determined that in order to define this thing we call Goth — for myself, my fellow Goths and the world at large — I must actually define the entire Gothdom. (Yes, that's a word. You can look that one up too.) And so here it is, a compilation and celebration of our obsessions, our heroes, our humour — and our hairstyles. Whether you're a Goth word geek like me, a friend/lover/parent of one or even just a writer trying to make characters more authentic, I hope this will be your guide to truly understanding this culture.

How to Use This Book

You'll note right away that this book has been organized alphabetically. That's because it's an encyclopedia. It contains more than 600 words and phrases used by Goths, covering what we listen to, watch and read; what we wear; where we hang out; what we talk about and much more, including more than 200 entries on influential Goth artists and personalities. Like all such books, it takes words very seriously. The list was prepared first and foremost through a lifetime of talking to, listening to and reading about Goths. Terms were cross-referenced with zines and books, websites and blogs, then tested on real live Goths to ensure accuracy and currency. That commitment to detail doesn't mean we can't have fun, and you'll certainly find snarky, melodramatic commentary, another hallmark of Gothdom. You are welcome to read it from A to Z but it is my hope that you'll simply dive in, perhaps with a favourite word, or one you've always been curious about. You'll notice that some parts of the descriptions are typeset DIFFERENTLY; this indicates a word or phrase that has its own entry for ease of cross-referencing. No doubt Goth readers will have fresh ideas of their own that I have overlooked, or perhaps even an argument for an error. I welcome such suggestions for potential future editions; write to liisa@encyclopediagothica.com. Meanwhile, I pray you will not read this book like an assignment, rather that you simply immerse yourself in it and delight in the black humour and decadent language that, truly, is What Is Goth.

ABSINTHE

ABSINTHE Liqueur of green colour and anise flavour distilled from wormwood, a potent psychedelic. Long favoured by Goths for its elegant preparation ritual and associations with madness, death and decadent creative types (POE, BAUDELAIRE, Wilde, etc.). Popularized in the 1990s after appearing in the NINE INCH NAILS video for "The Perfect Drug" and POPPY Z. BRITE's novel *Lost Souls*. Also known as "The Green Fairy" or "La fée verte."

ABYSS, AZRAEL Fictional co-host of GOTH TALK, a cable access TV spoof produced as a recurring sketch on *Saturday Night Live* (1997–1999). Portrayed by comedian Chris Kattan, he was the melodramatic Goth persona of high school student Todd Henderson, who worked a MUNDANE day job at CINNABON and tried to avoid beatings by his jock brother. Sporting cliché white face make-up, black clothing and BACKCOMBED hair, he spoke in a high-pitched voice, often screeched like a cat and signed off with "Stay out of the daylight!"

ADDAMS FAMILY, THE Fictional "creepy and kooky" family created by American cartoonist Charles Addams in the 1930s. Father Gomez, mother MORTICIA, daughter WEDNESDAY, son Pugsley, Uncle Fester and Cousin Itt were obsessed with the macabre and displayed a funereal style that could be considered proto-Goth. (The Addams Family Mansion has inspired many a home décor project.) Originally appearing as a cartoon in *The New Yorker* and adapted for several films in the 1990s, the clan's most beloved incarnation remains the black-and-white TV series (1964–1966), featuring its trademark theme song composed by Vic Mizzy. *See also: Munsters, The*

AGF Abbreviation for alt.gothic.fashion, a Usenet group for the discussion of Goth fashion and beauty that splintered off from ALT.GOTHIC in 1995 after one too many posts about pointy shoes. Typical post subjects: "How can I keep my clothes black?" or "How do I make a PARASOL?" At one point, it was used to identify community members in other online activities (e.g., including AGF in the title of an eBay auction). Members may be referred to as AGF-ers, although this is, like those baggy TRIPP pants, quite out of style.

ALCHEMY GOTHIC Jewelry design company founded in 1977 by British punks Geoff Kayson and Trevor Phillipson. Their MEDIEVAL-inspired pewter pieces were an immediate hit with '80s Goths, rockers and bikers alike; soon Alchemy became the go-to gang for spiders, skulls, bones and BATS on rings, necklaces and such. Having since expanded their empire to include clothing and lifestyle items (SILVER dragon goblet or ABSINTHE glassware set, anyone?), Alchemy's signature styles remain rooted in historical, Ye Olde English designs, from Victoriana to STEAMPUNK.

ALIEN SEX FIEND British GOTHIC ROCK band formed in 1982 in London. Generally considered the ultimate representation of the early '80s BATCAVE sound and style, so named for the first POST-PUNK nightclub night in London, at which singer Nik Fiend worked and ASF regularly performed. Fiend is best known for his horror-themed appearance, including ghoulish face make-up and FISHNET clothing. Hits include "Now I'm Feeling Zombified" and a cover of Johnny Cash's "I Walk the Line." *See also: Specimen*

ALLEY, THE Chicago indoor mall of alternative retailers, offering more than 40,000 square feet of T-shirts, boots, jewelry, leather goods and other hallmarks of subcultural style at the corner of Belmont and Clark streets. Yes, you can buy this stuff cheaper at HOT TOPIC, and yes, RECOVERING GOTHS and other adults may not appreciate the punker-than-thou attitude of some staff, and no, it might not be the best place to get an extreme piercing or TATTOO. But many a teen has been very happily outfitted here. And they used to have a COFFIN in the shop full of band pins. (On a personal note, I bought the best pair of LATEX stiletto boots ever on sale here once. Thanks!)

ALT.GOTHIC Usenet group dedicated to the general discussion of Goth culture, founded (around HALLOWEEN

1991) as a spinoff of Dominion, the electronic mailing list for THE SISTERS OF MERCY. In general, Goths were early adopters of the net, and the forum acted as a social hub for hitherto far-flung FREAKS of all persuasions to discuss music, fashion, art as well as those Big Questions about life and death. Alt.gothic became the repository of much Goth news and lore and a significant source of slang, in-jokes, etc. Members launched the annual CONVERGENCE convention, which they organized when not busy typing catty replies to the question "Is MARILYN MANSON Goth?" In 1995, separate groups were created for Brits (uk.people.gothic) and fashion (alt.gothic.fashion). Like most such newsgroups, its use and influence have dwindled since the rise of social networks. *See also: Net.goth*

AMBIENT Musical genre encompassing a wide range of styles, most of them instrumental and electronic in nature, with an emphasis on atmosphere and non-musical elements, as popularized by Brian Eno in the 1970s and in chillout rooms at 1990s raves. More experimental ambient music is often sold by the same mail-order catalogues as underground Goth/Industrial records, and Goths often describe certain bands of a softer, more "exotic" nature — DEAD CAN DANCE, for example — as ambient, but it's not quite accurate to compare or confuse them. *See also: Dark ambient*

AMERICAN GOTHIC Despite its title and the prominent presence of a pitchfork, this iconic 1930 painting of

rural America by Grant Wood is not Goth. The production company for Chicago DJ Scary Lady Sarah
is though.

ANDROGYNY Blame it on Bowie and Bauhaus, but
boys have been donning make-up and ladies' fishnets
since before Goth was even called Goth. So common
a sight is males pinching feminine style that nobody
would bat a heavily mascaraed eyelash at boys in black
eyeliner, nailpolish or even a corset at a Goth bar.
Furthermore, few would assume anything about their
sexual orientation as a result. Academics muse on
how guys in skirts form part of Goth's overall gender
transgressions while those in question simply enjoy
the ritual of dressing up with friends of any gender
and pissing off most jocks and parents.

ANKH Ancient Egyptian hieroglyphic symbol for eternal life, displayed as a cross with an oval head. Ever
since David Bowie's character whipped out a gold
ankh pendant especially designed with a blade to slice
into necks in the horror flick *The Hunger*, it's been
especially associated with vampires. A must-have in
every wannabe vamp's chest of jewels.

ANNE RICE VAMPIRE LESTAT FAN CLUB As it sounds, a
fan club for author Anne Rice and her vampire chronicles. Formed in 1988 in New Orleans, the ARVLFC's
greatest contribution to Gothdom was producing the
annual Vampires Ball, a lavishly themed costume party

which gave you an excuse to buy that $1,000 velvet cloak you've always wanted.

ANT, ADAM British singer (né Stuart Leslie Goddard, b. November 3, 1954). Leader of punk band Adam and the Ants (1977–1982) and best known for 1982's #1 hit song "Goody Two Shoes." Ant personified the NEW ROMANTIC era of ANDROGYNOUS, glammed-up pop music. His pirate costumes, a suggestion of manager Malcolm McLaren, were probably responsible for the spread of POET SHIRTS to America.

APOPTYGMA BERZERK Norwegian INDUSTRIAL band formed by Stephan Groth in 1991, sometimes abbreviated as Apop. Alongside VNV NATION, part of the first wave of European acts mixing EBM with melodic SYNTHPOP that conquered North America's club playlists in the early 2000s, mostly through re-releases on METROPOLIS RECORDS. Peaked with 2002 album *Harmonizer*, but continue to enjoy heavy rotation at CYBERGOTH events.

AQUA NET Brand of American aerosol hairspray favoured by those wanting exceptionally strong hold at a budget price. Popularized during the 1980s for use on mohawks, DEATHHAWKS and other extreme styles requiring its tortoise-like shellac.

ASH, DANIEL British guitarist and singer (b. July 31, 1957), founder of Original Goth band BAUHAUS and its off-shoots TONES ON TAIL and LOVE AND ROCKETS. Atmosphere and aggression are his musical trademarks, plus spiked hair and a penchant for psychedelia. His solo albums never quite hit the charts, but with the royalties from his bands' "BELA LUGOSI'S DEAD" and "Go!" he can enjoy a life of leisure and occasional stints as a special guest DJ. His latest release is the 2009 solo EP *It's a Burn Out*.

ASTBURY, IAN British singer (b. May 14, 1962) best known as leader of THE CULT. Wolf child, howler of hymns, shaker of hips and tambourines, Astbury is one of many credited with the first use of the word Goth in a musical context, although by the time he called singer Andi Sex Gang and his followers "Goth" in 1982, the term was already in use so it's probably a bit revisionist on his part. His contributions instead came from writing classic songs like "She Sells Sanctuary" and making it acceptable to wear aviator sunglasses and fur hats to a Goth show. Less influential: his post-Cult project Holy Barbarians and a stint fronting The Doors ("of the 21st Century"). Still, the man's got attitude, soul and a vocal style that's unmatched. Don't count him out for a resurrection.

AUTUMN, EMILIE American singer and violinist (née Emilie Autumn Liddell, b. September 22, 1979). A self-proclaimed Wayward Victorian Girl, her vaudevillian performances and songs about asylums have attracted a rabid fanbase of young girls into striped tights, brightly coloured hair and heavy metal–type vocal screeching over INDUSTRIAL beats. Her debut CD, *Enchant*, was released in 2002 and has become a kind of classic for the kids. She has performed with rock stars like Courtney Love and Billy Corgan, not that her legions would be particularly impressed by that. No, they like her for being a Goth Girl for their generation, not so much related to HAMMER HORROR and punk rock as to anime and cabaret. She's very cute.

BAUHAUS

BABYBAT A newcomer to the scene exhibiting limited knowledge, particularly one of a young age; sometimes used derogatorily. Alternatively, a term of endearment for underage Goths. *Compare: Kindergoth*

BABY, THE STARS SHINE BRIGHT Japanese fashion label created by Akinori and Fumiyo Isobe, credited with kickstarting the GOTHIC LOLITA style in 1988. Think babydolls and PARASOLS, with lots of lace. TRAD GOTHS may find it difficult to imagine how a powder blue outfit could appeal to anyone, but for enthusiasts of Loli lifestyle, Baby is the best. Retail outlets in Paris and San Francisco satisfy the foreign fans; the HQ is in Shibuya, Tokyo.

BACKCOMBING Hairstyling technique also known as teasing where you grab a chunk of hair and aggressively comb backwards until it hurts too much or the hair stands high up on its own, whichever comes first. Add illogical amounts of AQUA NET hairspray and — voila! — instant ROBERT SMITH or SIOUXSIE SIOUX 'do.

BADDELEY, GAVIN British journalist (b. 1966), author of books on Goths, Satanism and Satanic Goths, including *Goth Chic: A Connoisseur's Guide to Dark Culture*; *Lucifer Rising: A Book of Sin, Devil Worship and Rock 'n' Roll*;

and *Goths: Vamps and Dandies*, as well as biographies of
MARILYN MANSON and CRADLE OF FILTH. An ordained
minister of the CHURCH OF SATAN, he's the go-to guy
whenever U.K. television producers need someone to
talk about the dark side who actually has a clue.

BAD SEEDS *See: Cave, Nick*

BAL DES VAMPIRES, LE Fancy costume ball produced
by San Francisco's Period Events and Entertainments
Recreation Society, held annually around HALLOWEEN.
An elegant affair featuring formal dancing to ba-
roque and waltz music, attracting ROMANTIGOTHS,
STEAMPUNKS and others who like to party like it's 1899.

BALK, FAIRUZA American actress (née Fairuza Alejandra
Feldthouse, b. May 21, 1974) best known for her starring role in the 1996 film *The Craft*, in which she played
a teen witch with rather Goth style. She projected a
dark, rock 'n' roll image in her real life as well — tat-
toed and pierced with black hair and copious EYELINER
— and Goths were thrilled to learn she once owned an
actual occult shop in Hollywood. In 2010, Balk announced a new music project, Armed Love Militia;
first single "Stormwinds" featured guest DAVID J.

BANSHEES, THE *See: Siouxsie and the Banshees*

BARA, THEDA American silent film star (née Theodise
Burr Goodman, 1885–1955). Nicknamed "The Vamp"

for her femme fatale performances, she wore provocative costumes and posed for occult-themed promotional photos with skulls and snakes. If that wasn't enough to secure her honorary Goth Girl status, her 1917 role as Cleopatra set the template for the Egyptian eye make-up popularized by SIOUXSIE SIOUX some sixty years later. Ashes interred at Forest Lawn Memorial Park columbarium in Glendale, California. *See also: Brooks, Louise*

BARELY EVIL Adult website offering porn pictorials of TATTOOED Goth Girls — pierced, bound, penetrated by machines. *See also: Blue Blood, Gothic Sluts*

BARGELD, BLIXA German singer and musician (né Hans Christian Emmerich, b. January 12, 1959). Co-founded seminal INDUSTRIAL noise group Einstürzende Neubauten in 1980. From 1983 to 2003, member of NICK CAVE's band, The Bad Seeds. Says he's not Goth, but ample photographic evidence of him in leather pants, BACKCOMBED hair or funereal suits crumpled like he just crawled out of a coffin proves otherwise.

BARKER, CLIVE British author, filmmaker and visual artist (b. October 5, 1952). The leading voice in contemporary horror fiction, revered for his gory and imaginative explorations of sexuality and the supernatural. His debut collection, *The Books of Blood* (1984–1985), so impressed STEPHEN KING, he called

Barker "the future of horror." Novella *The Hellbound Heart* (adapted into film as HELLRAISER) introduced the CENOBITES — a gang of interdimensional sadomasochistic demons with body piercings and mutilations.

BAT Flying mammal, patron animal of Goths. Maybe it's because they're nocturnal and live in caves. Or maybe it's because some of them drink blood for dinner or, as film legend has it, turn into VAMPIRES. But these tiny webbed and wingèd creatures have come to symbolize us, and in turn we've adopted them as our fantasy pets, designing purses in their shape, TATTOOING their image on our bodies, channelling their spirit while dancing. Guano aside, if we could live in a batcave, we probably would. *See also: I'm So Goth, Vampire bats*

BATCAVE 1. Nightclub operating in London, ENGLAND, from 1982 to 1986. Famed as the world's first Goth bar, although originally dedicated to NEW WAVE and glam rock and other fashion-conscious offshoots of punk. Before the term "Goth" was used to describe its death-obsessed crowd or their music, regulars were referred to as "Batcavers." Soon-to-be-Goth luminaries such as SIOUXSIE SIOUX, ROBERT SMITH and NICK CAVE regularly attended for live performances by SPECIMEN or ALIEN SEX FIEND, or to just watch scary art movies. 2. Contemporary GOTHIC ROCK groups that look and sound like Alien Sex Fiend, mostly from Europe. 3. Lair of comic book superhero Batman, coveted by many. 4. An actual cave of BATS; great spot for a first date.

BAT CONSERVATION INTERNATIONAL Charitable organization based in Austin, Texas, that protects BATS and their habitats all around the world and provides tips for attracting bats to your very own bat house! Many individual Goths participate in their adopt-a-bat program, and it's common for businesses and events to donate funds to the org.

BÁTHORY, ELIZABETH Hungarian countess (1560–1614) and serial killer also known as the Blood Countess. Accused of torturing and murdering hundreds of young females, she was imprisoned in her own castle until her death. Stories of her bathing in the blood of virgins as a fountain of youth are legendary and have given rise to the myth of Báthory as a VAMPIRE, exploited in such horror films as *Countess Dracula* (1971). Despite the gruesomeness of her alleged crimes (or perhaps because of it), her influence on Goth types is unabated: the Báthory name has been used by a Swedish black metal band, a Goth clothing shop in Belgium and as a pseudonym for countless teen girl bloggers worldwide.

BATS DAY Gathering of gothy types at Disneyland in Anaheim, California, held annually since 1999. Attracts up to 2,000 spookily clad kids of all ages; activities include posing for group photos with Sleeping Beauty's castle, hogging the HAUNTED MANSION ride, stalking the Evil Queen and otherwise painting the Happiest Place on Earth black and red. Needless to say, not an official Disney-sanctioned event.

BATWING Type of sleeve used in Gothic blouses or dresses in which the arms, when outstretched, look like webbed BAT wings. Not to be confused with the traditional batwing sleeve of the disco era, in which a large armhole and tapered wrists provide a handglider look.

BAUDELAIRE, CHARLES French poet and critic (1821–1867) whose writings were as decadent as his lifestyle. The poetry collection *Les Fleurs du Mal* (*The Flowers of Evil*, 1857) caused a scandal with its blasphemous musings on sex and death, drawn perhaps from his own dalliances with prostitutes, drunks and other scoundrels. A fan of Gothic texts and EDGAR ALLAN POE in particular, he is credited for introducing Poe to Europe by way of his French translations, and Baudelaire remains an inspiration to wannabe dark poets and DANDIES everywhere. Buried at Montparnasse Cemetery in Paris, which also houses a cenotaph monument to him.

BAUHAUS British GOTHIC ROCK band formed in 1978 by horror and art aficionados PETER MURPHY (vocals), DANIEL ASH (guitars), KEVIN HASKINS (drums) and DAVID J. (bass). Considered the first pure Goth band, thanks to its combination of ghastly image, Murphy's baritone vocals, macabre and dramatic live performances and a debut single about horror icon

BELA LUGOSI. After three albums that were underappreciated by the press and a Top 20 single in Britain with a cover of DAVID BOWIE's "Ziggy Stardust," group disbanded in 1983 to pursue solo and side-projects. Reunited in 1998 and again in 2005; released alleged final album in 2008. One of the most influential musical acts to emerge from the POST-PUNK era of any genre, Bauhaus is primarily upheld alongside THE SISTERS OF MERCY and THE CURE as the most revered acts in all of English Gothdom (despite members' insistence that they are not Goth, which of course is a sure sign that they are). *See also: Bela Lugosi's Dead; Love and Rockets; Tones on Tail*

BAUHEARSEMOBILE Hearse purchased by members of BAUHAUS as a touring vehicle from an undertaker during the recording sessions for *The Sky's Gone Out* in 1981. Despite its obvious visual appeal, couldn't really handle the job, and after pushing it up a hill one too many times they sold it off.

BDSM Abbreviation for bondage, domination, sado-masochism, a complex variety of sexual practices and fetishes exploring pleasure and pain, of particular interest to many Goths as lifestyle and/or fashion. Since VIVIENNE WESTWOOD designed BONDAGE PANTS for punk rockers in 1970s London, typical dungeon equipment such as handcuffs, straps and chains have been incorporated into Goth/Industrial clothing designs. Nightclubs commonly hold special events catering to this scene;

BDSM may be listed as acceptable apparel in the strict dress code. Not all Goths participate, and even those dressed in whips and chains may have little knowledge of or interest in actual BDSM. *See also: Fetish night*

BEGGARS BANQUET British record label founded by Martin Mills and Nick Austin in 1977, originally to release punk rock vinyl but later home to THE CULT, Gary Numan, BAUHAUS and many others.

B.E. GOTH *See: Bleeding edge Goth*

BELA LUGOSI'S DEAD First and most famous GOTHIC ROCK song, written and recorded by BAUHAUS and released as the band's debut single as a white vinyl 12" limited to 5,000 copies in August 1979. A nine-minute, experimental, minimalist howl dedicated to the man who played the most famous DRACULA in all of cinema, anchored by the chorus "undead, undead, undead." Used to great effect in Tony Scott's 1983 VAMPIRE film *THE HUNGER* (in which the band — well, mostly singer PETER MURPHY — appears performing in a cage). It did not hit the charts at the time but has become a club, party and HALLOWEEN-wedding standard, the perfect soundtrack for fog-filled dance floors everywhere.

BELLA GOTH Virtual Goth Girl character in the *SimCity* universe. Not to be confused with Bella Swan of the TWILIGHT universe.

BELLA MORTE American DARKWAVE band, formed in 1996 in Charlottesville, Virginia, by singer Andy Deane and bassist Gopal Metro. Originally independent, they signed to CLEOPATRA RECORDS and then METROPOLIS RECORDS and have enjoyed some underground success alongside the new crop of gothic rockers, with an accessible mix of DEATH ROCK guitars and SYNTHPOP, HORROR PUNK stylings and tortured romantic lyrics that would probably be on alternative radio if they had a bigger production budget. Deane is also a DJ and author who has published several horror novels.

BERGER, FRED H. American fetish photographer and magazine publisher, founder of influential 1980s magazine PROPAGANDA, for which he supplied a steady stream of black-and-white images of ANDROGYNOUS Goth Boys languishing prettily in graveyards or flirting with fascist fashion iconography. More recently, published photography books *Pulp Fetish* and *Desperados: A Homographic Portfolio*, but otherwise seems to have fallen off the grid.

BIRTHDAY MASSACRE, THE Canadian synthrock band formed in 1999 in London, Ontario, and lead by the PERKY GOTH singer Chibi. The band's colourful pop sensibilities and fairytale-like narratives caught on quickly with a young audience, who discovered the band on social networks such as MySpace and VAMPIREFREAKS. With a global fanbase, record deal with METROPOLIS RECORDS and a new harder-edged sound, the band is poised to weather its growing pains into adulthood quite well. Key tracks: "Red Stars" and "Looking Glass" from the 2007 album *Walking with Strangers*.

BIRTHDAY PARTY Australian POST-PUNK band formed in 1980 by singer NICK CAVE and guitarist Mick Harvey, later relocating to London and Berlin. Legendary purveyors of menacing noise and shrieking vocals drawing inspiration from shock rock, blues, No WAVE and hard drugs. Often considered early torchbearers of GOTHIC ROCK, their brand of sonic terror directly influenced the early BATCAVE bands and DEATH ROCKERS before the band self-destructed in 1983. Nick Cave went on to great success with The Bad Seeds. Essential tracks include "Release the Bats," "Dead Joe" and a cover of "Jack the Ripper."

BITE ME Scottish magazine devoted to all things vampiric, launched by Arlene Russo in 1999. The full-size, glossy publication covers supernatural lore, modern movies, spooky events around the world, Goth babes and more. Russo has also authored an exposé of "real" VAMPIRES, *Vampire Nation*.

BLACK The colour of night, the absence of light, the heart of a Goth. All of our lives, we are asked, "Why do you wear all black?" Maybe we're in mourning for the world. Maybe, like Einstein, we like a wardrobe that's easy to match. It's kind of like asking a unicorn why it has a horn. Some things just are.

BLACKLIGHT Type of ultraviolet lighting commonly used in nightclubs to show off specially designed glow-in-the-dark or reflective CYBERGOTH clothing, special effects make-up, white cat hairs and dandruff.

BLACK NO. 1 Song by Brooklyn GOTHIC METAL band TYPE O NEGATIVE, from the album *Bloody Kisses* (1993) and titled in full "Black No. 1 (Little Miss Scare All)." A sarcastic ode to Goth Girls based on a narcissist ex-girlfriend of singer PETER STEELE, cheekily referencing Lily MUNSTER and NOSFERATU and featuring a refrain about loving the dead. Title references a common product number for black hair dye.

BLACK PHOENIX ALCHEMY LAB Brand of perfumes and essential oils created by Elizabeth Moriaty Barrial and Brian Constantine, often called BPAL. Their on-line apothecary offers concoctions named Bewitched, Voodoo, Ode on Melancholy and the like, with ingredients such as "black rose, olibanum, dark musk, myrrh, blackcurrant, lavender buds, bourbon geranium and amber incense." Lines have been created based on the works of NEIL GAIMAN and Gris Grimly. Their packaging is romantic and VICTORIAN, perfect for collecting or trading.

BLACK ROSE British retailer of Goth and punk clothing and accessories, launched in CAMDEN MARKET in London in 1994 and now operating as a successful online mail-order business.

BLACK TAPE FOR A BLUE GIRL American DARKWAVE group formed in 1986 by songwriter Sam Rosenthal, founder of PROJEKT RECORDS. Evolving from electronic soundscapes to ETHEREAL to a more DARK CABARET style over the course of its ten albums, it features a rotating cast of male and female vocalists and the overarching theme of seduction, both lyrically and sonically. Rosenthal has made good use of the Projekt networks to get BTFABG in front of the entire Goth nation, making them one of the most prominent and longstanding indie bands in the scene.

BLEEDING EDGE GOTHS Brand of dolls and action figures featuring gothy, witchy, vampy types molded in miniature plastic, painted with the appropriate piercings, TATTOOS and clubwear and assigned cliché personality traits. ("VeroniKa Despair" likes boat rides on lakes after dark.) Sold as limited-edition collectibles through membership in the company's Crypt Club.

BLEEP General term for electronic music played at a Goth club that annoys the TRAD GOTHS and death rockers, used almost exclusively in the U.K. So-named for the "bleepy" room at London's SLIMELIGHT club which played EBM, electro and other genres of interest to the CYBERGOTHS, who are sometimes called "bleepy." Some Goth bars snidely advertise their more rock-oriented playlists as "bleep-free."

BLOWFISH Someone wearing an abundance of spiked clothing, jewelry or accessories, thus resembling a blowfish. Not widely used.

BLUE BLOOD American adult magazine founded 1992, dedicated to counterculture fashion, art and sex. Prior to internet sites such as SUICIDE GIRLS, it was one of first media outlets to promote pierced, TATTOOED ladies as pin-up models in erotic pictorials often featuring VAMPIRE or BDSM themes. Has since expanded its alt.porn empire with the much-less-subtly named websites GOTHIC SLUTS and Rubber Dollies.

BLUE NUN German wine, popular with some Goths because WAYNE HUSSEY from THE MISSION used to drink it on stage all the time.

BME Short for Body Mod Ezine.

BODY MODS Short form for body modifications, the act of deliberately altering the human body for ritual, rite of passage, sexual gratification or fashion, either permanently or semi-permanently. Such common practices as piercing, TATTOOING or branding are all body mods. Popular Goth mods include facial piercings, genital piercings and scarification. More extreme mods such as tongue splitting, flesh hook suspension, subdermal implants (especially horns) and filing of the teeth into fang-like points are rare but generally considered attractive. *See also: Modern primitives*

BONDAGE BELT Belt used traditionally in sexual play as a restraint tool, which has been adapted as a fashion accessory. Commonly made of leather and affixed with assorted D-RINGS and chains that can either be attached to cuffs or left to make that jingle-jangle sound that signals one's arrival, not unlike a cowbell. A bitch at airport security.

BONDAGE PANTS Pants affixed with any combination of zippers, chains, studs and buckles and generally featuring removable straps or braces — none of which serve any practical purpose. Introduced to U.K. punks in the late 1970s by designer VIVIENNE WESTWOOD's boutique SEX and traditionally produced in a tartan print. American designers TRIPP NYC updated the look in the 1990s, creating a low-rise, wide-legged pant with expandable zip legs and oversized pockets, widely sold at the HOT TOPIC retail chain and popular with young RIVETHEADS and GRAVERS.

BOOK OF SHADOWS In the WICCA religion, a book of sacred and magical spells. Originally ascribed to a specific book written by English ringleader Gerard Gardner in the 1950s, or one passed ritualistically amongst the coven by the High Priest or Priestess, now commonly used for a personal journal where any practitioner keeps records of his/her spells. Popularized for contemporary non-Wiccans by its use on the television series *Charmed* and the film *The Craft*. *Compare: Grimoire*

BOWIE, DAVID British singer and actor (né David Robert Jones, b. January 8, 1947) whose theatrical stage personas often skirt or flirt with outright Gothdom. His ANDROGYNOUS, alien alter ego Ziggy Stardust, and the accompanying concept album *The Rise and Fall of Ziggy Stardust and the Spiders from Mars* (1972), was ripped off by many a glam boy including MARILYN MANSON; title track covered famously by BAUHAUS. Embraced INDUSTRIAL music on *Outside* (1995), complete with enlisting NINE INCH NAILS' Trent Reznor for remixing and tour support. His performance as an aging VAMPIRE in the film THE HUNGER (1983) remains one of the most memorable and erotic bloodsuckers on film. Whatever characters he devises next, his spot in ELDER GOTH Hall of Fame is secure.

BOY LONDON British streetwear company founded in 1977 as a punk shop on King's Road in London peddling bondage wear and T-shirts. Best known for its bold "BOY London" logo and unabashed use of German WWII eagle iconography. Mail-order catalogue also made skull buckle boots, POET SHIRTS and other early Goth apparel available to wannabe death rockers everywhere. Jonny Slut of the BATCAVE band SPECIMEN was a model.

BRAN CASTLE A thirteenth-century fortress in Romania associated with VLAD TEPES and marketed as "DRACULA's Castle" to tourists. Your long-dreamed-of Transylvanian getaway will no doubt include plenty of time in its gift shop.

BRITE, POPPY Z. American author (née Melissa Ann Brite, b. May 25, 1967) based in New Orleans. Debut novel, *Lost Souls* (1992), was the most influential VAM-PIRE book post—ANNE RICE and pre—Stephenie Meyer, launching a new style of gothic horror filled with rock 'n' roll, gay characters and actual, authentically imagined Goths (e.g., they smoked CLOVES). The fol-low-ups *Drawing Blood* (1993) and *Exquisite Corpse* (1996) also explored the supernatural, the occult, bisexual-ity, hackers, serial killers and cannibals. Brite edited two erotic vampire anthologies, *Love in Vein* and *Twice Bitten: Love in Vein II*. One of his many short stories, "The Sixth Sentinel," was adapted for an episode of the TV horror anthology *The Hunger*. Has since aban-doned horror writing for a series of dark comedies about the restaurant world. Maintains an active LiveJournal where he blogs about his new work and personal life, including his experience with gender reassignment.

BROOKS, LOUISE American silent film actress, model, dancer and showgirl (née Mary Louise Brooks, 1906–1985) famed in her day as a globe-trotting heartbreaker and all round vamp. Considered by many the first Goth-styled pop icon. Her famous dark bob hairstyle — short, sharp and straight — adopted and adapted by many a Goth Girl who remembers that one of Miss Brooks' other known characteristics was to never smile in photographs. GOTH POINTS: +50. Buried in Holy Sepulchre Cemetery, Rochester, New York.

BUCKLE BOOTS Any boot featuring a superfluous number of buckles on the side, either as closure or adornment, although traditionally referring to a flat-soled, ankle-high leather boot with extremely pointed toes. Platforms, stilettos or army boots can all be gothified with a few more buckles, which may include skulls, BATS, pentagrams or spiders. A Goth closet standard. *See also: Demonia, New Rock, Transmuter, Winkle pickers*

BUFFY THE VAMPIRE SLAYER American TV series (1997–2003) created by Joss Whedon based on his 1992 film of the same name and starring Sarah Michelle Gellar as Buffy Summers, a high-school student and Slayer of VAMPIRES, demons and assorted "baddies." Not specifically Goth, although with the story's focus on the supernatural and the occult, was embraced by many. Sexy vampire protagonists didn't hurt either. *See also: Evil Willow*

BULLET BELT Belt made from a string of used bullet casings, worn on the hips by both boys and girls of the Goth, punk and metal variety. Sold in a variety of calibres and colours, all of which are very heavy metal.

BURTON, TIM American filmmaker and author (b. August 25, 1958). His work defined Gothic style and storytelling in the late twentieth century, visualizing dark dreamworlds filled with endearing misfits in macabre scenarios (and striped tights) — then exposing them to the mainstream masses via Hollywood block-busters. Almost all of his films feature Goth characters or themes, including *Beetlejuice* (1988), *Batman* (1989), *EDWARD SCISSORHANDS* (1990), *Sleepy Hollow* (1999) and *Sweeney Todd* (2007) and the stop-motion animated features *THE NIGHTMARE BEFORE CHRISTMAS* (1993) and *Corpse Bride* (2005). His first short film, "Vincent," was a tribute to horror film icon VINCENT PRICE, about whom he has a long-delayed documentary in development. His signature style is both ghoulish and whimsical, closer to modern fairytales than hard horror; its influence can be seen in fashion, drawing and design the world over, much of it referred to as "Burtonesque."

BUSH, KATE British singer (b. July 30, 1958) whose 1978 chart-topping debut single "Wuthering Heights" — an ethereal interpretation of Emily Brontë's romantic ghost story — is one of the purest expressions of the Gothic in popular music. An ode to HAMMER HORROR followed too, then a successful career as an artful popstar who is rarely referenced in the Goth canon but makes music perfect for haunting moors.

BYRON, LORD British poet (né George Gordon Byron, 1788–1824). Hero of the Romantic movement and romanticized still for his tumultuous and scandalous love affairs with both men and women. Famous to Goths by association with writers Percy Bysshe SHELLEY, Mary Shelley and JOHN POLIDORI. In 1816 in a villa on Lake Geneva, Switzerland, the gang participated in some legendary late night telling of fantastic stories, from which sprung the horror classics *FRANKENSTEIN* and *The Vampyre*. Has appeared in many fictional accounts of the era, none so seductive as the feature film *Gothic* (1986) starring Gabriel Byrne as the Lord. His remains were rejected by Westminster Abbey for burial; they rest instead at Church of St. Mary Magdalene in Hucknall, Nottinghamshire.

CANDELABRA

CABARET VOLTAIRE British electronic music trio formed in Sheffield, ENGLAND, in 1973 by Stephen Mallinder, Richard H. Kirk and Chris Watson. Named for a Swiss nightclub with Dadaist ties, these early experimenters with tape loops and sound art are often listed as a seminal INDUSTRIAL band, but their most well-known tracks are pure SYNTHPOP, for example 1984's hypnotic "Sensoria."

CAMDEN MARKET Group of adjoining open-air markets on Regent's Canal north of central London, U.K., selling food, knick-knacks and more Goth/ CYBERGOTH/vintage clothing than you can shake a glow-in-the-dark VICTORIAN walking stick at. Amongst the permanent indoor shops of the Stables Market beckoning children of the night are those famous ones with names like After Dark, Elizium, FAIRYGOTHMOTHER, Darkside, CYBERDOG and, um, Pink Fluffy. A one-stop shopping experience from head to pointy toe.

CANDELABRA Electricity is so overrated. While the rest of the world has mostly abandoned the candelabra for lightbulbs or fat pillar candles, Goths can still be seen stalking about their abodes clutching the multi-candle holder (more likely made from wrought iron than traditional brass) trying to keep the wax from dripping onto their lacy POET SHIRT sleeves. A perfect house-warming gift.

CANDI, RAZOR American model (née Kym McLaughlin, b. 1983) currently based in Romania. Starting out a go-go dancer in the mid 1990s at Florida's largest Goth club, The Castle, then doing runway fashion shows and shoots for mags such as DROP DEAD and GOTHIC BEAUTY. Recognizable for her black DEATH-HAWK and other extreme looks, she was alternative even in the alternative modeling world. Has released books of her most memorable photos.

CAPE Despite what the packaging on VAMPIRE HALL-OWEEN costumes say, DRACULA does not wear a cape. Superman wears a cape. *Compare: Cloak*

CARMILLA VAMPIRE novel by Joseph Sheridan le Fanu, published in 1872. Pre-dating DRACULA by twenty-five years, it may have influenced STOKER's classic book, but that's not why it's famous. With its titular female predator and her young lady lover, it became the template for lesbian vampires, influencing hundreds of sexy stories ever since, HAMMER's 1970 film *The Vampire Lovers* for just one example. British black metal band CRADLE OF FILTH's 1996 album, *Dusk . . . and Her Embrace*, is inspired by the tale.

CARNIVAL OF SOULS 1. British Goth/fetish club event started in London in 1994 by a chap named Fulani and running biannually at the Zanzibar club from 2006 to 2008. Much dressing up (and some dressing-downs) ensued. 2. Cult status low-budget horror film from 1962 directed by Herk Harvey and starring Candace Hilligoss, a great organ score by Gene Moore and a creepy amusement park.

CARPE NOCTEM American magazine published from 1993 to 2000 by Thom Cornell and Catia Carnell; name translates from Latin to "seize the night." A glossy zine with significant distribution, it covered music, film, books and art from the dark side, interviewing big names in then-underground culture from CLIVE BARKER to DIAMANDA GÁLAS (as well as a then-unknown musician/magician named Criss Angel), and featuring original fiction and art, including the earliest publication of Jhonen Vasquez's comic *JOHNNY THE HOMICIDAL MANIAC*.

CARPE NOCTURNE American magazine, founded in 2004 by editor Bob Donovan as a monthly print publication. Carrying the torch in the new millennium with coverage of the Goth/INDUSTRIAL/EBM/ SYNTHPOP/STEAMPUNK scene, focused heavily on music with some coverage of fashion, comics and body art. After a hiatus in 2008, returned in 2010 as a quarterly digital magazine.

CASH, JOHNNY American country singer (1932–2003), a.k.a. The Man in Black, whose music you won't hear at a Goth club but who you might find on the iPods of those who appreciate his gruesome murder ballads, his sorrowful gospel numbers, his bad-ass rockabilly and his commitment to an all-black wardrobe. At the very least, they'll know his song "I Walk the Line" (covered by ALIEN SEX FIEND) and his 2002 cover of NINE INCH NAILS' "Hurt."

CATACOMBS Underground burial chambers of ancient origin and much beloved by the type of modern traveller who likes to holiday amongst the dead. Catacombs are open for visits in Rome, Egypt and elsewhere, but none more spectacular than those winding deep beneath the streets of Paris, where the walls are made from thousands of skulls and bones greeting those who dare pass through the stone portal bearing the warning *"Arrête, c'est ici l'empire de la mort."* Rumours abound of off-the-path wanderings and illegal parties within the Parisian Catacombs; in September 2009, vandalism forced their closure for a year. Tsk, tsk. Extra GOTH POINTS for knowing this type of tomb is actually called an ossuary.

CATALYST, CLINT American author and performer (né Clinton Green, b. April 8, 1971) and all-around gay Goth scenester. From his zine *As If* in the early 1990s to his 2000 book *Cottonmouth Kisses*, his spoken word performances, journalism, modeling, acting and many other gigs, he has constantly put himself out there, his way. Recently, he has taken an interest in reality

TV; amongst his credits is guesting on an episode of *Germany's Next Top Model*. A real life modern DANDY.

CAT O' NINE TAILS Flogging device, often of rope or leather, with nine "thongs," also called the Captain's Daughter by navy types. Catwoman had one. Anita Blake too. Whether or not you like to Whip It, a striking accessory.

CAVE, NICK Australian-born singer, composer and author (b. September 22, 1957), now based in the U.K. As frontman for POST-PUNK pioneers THE BIRTHDAY PARTY, introduced himself as a young man obsessed with religion, sex, violence and self-destruction. Thankfully, outlived the self-destruction part so he could go on to front Nick Cave and the Bad Seeds and release more than a dozen albums filled with murder ballads, dark romance and ruminations on religion and other heady offerings, writ like a poet, sung like the devil. His 1989 novel *And the Ass Saw the Angel* was pure Southern Gothic; the 2009 follow-up *The Death of Bunny Munro* was perverse and hilarious. He scored the apocalyptic 2009 masterpiece *The Road*; wrote 2005's nasty Outback Western *The Proposition*. His latest band Grinderman rocks. His canon is literary and seductive. His suits are sharp. Not obviously Goth but at some point in every Goth girl or boy's life, they discover Nick Cave. Then there is no turning back. Essential tracks: "The Mercy Seat," "The Ship Song," "Red Right Hand," "Where the Wild Roses Grow,"

"Stagger Lee," "Spell" . . . oh hell, just get the whole Bad Seeds catalogue.

CBGB New York City bar and live music venue, operating in the Bowery district from 1973 to 2006. While world famous as the birthplace of American punk rock, and mostly home to hardcore and metal and a really, really stinky washroom, it was also the original spot for weekly Goth party Absolution, and many a death rocker met his/her soulmate there amongst the ruins.

CEMETERY Burial ground for the dead, gathering place for the death-obsessed. Various superstitions and legend say it's where ZOMBIES will rise, devils should be worshipped and, of course, VAMPIRES may rest. Whether any of that is true, they still make lovely places for a quiet stroll thinking about mortality, practicing your black-and-white photography and GRAVE RUBBING art projects or, the ultimate Goth date, moonlit sex romps on graves. If you hear about tortured cats and wax pentagrams messing up your local cemetery, chances are that's a misguided teenager, not a Goth.

CENOBITES Fictional BDSM-loving creatures from another dimension, created by CLIVE BARKER and stars of his HELLRAISER stories and film. An entire canon of philosophy and abilities exists for the Cenobites, but few would care if they didn't look so incredibly cool. Well, cool in that "we'll tear your soul apart" way. Mutilated, pierced, TATTOOED, decked out in part—religious vestment part—fetish gear, Cenobites both repulse and titillate. Barker's fever dreams made flesh. *See also: Pinhead*

CENOTAPH Tomb or monument for a person or group of persons buried elsewhere. Generally used to honour the war dead, and thus quite a sombre affair. But in the absence of a handy CEMETERY, a perfectly suitable back-up for late night Goth walks.

CHAINMAIL A type of MESH formed from metal rings linked together, which can be fashioned into shirts, gloves, etc. For some reason, many Goth boys go through a phase where wearing chainmail out to clubs seems like a good idea. Chainmail was designed as armour, to protect against getting stabbed while attacking enemy tribes on your horse, so if you are recreating such a thing in a LARP game, by all means, get yourself some chainmail. If not, leave it to the butchers and the shark divers, won't you?

CHILDREN OF THE NIGHT *"Listen to them. Children of the night. What music they make,"* quoth Count DRACULA in BRAM STOKER's novel, in reference to howling wolves in the hills around his castle. Since then, there have been films, short stories, songs and more riffing on the idea, and Goths eagerly embracing it as a term of endearment.

CHRISTIAN DEATH American DEATH ROCK band, founded in 1979 in Los Angeles by singer ROZZ

WILLIAMS, whose impact on Gothdom cannot be understated, despite never having enjoyed a chart hit. Debut studio album, 1982's *Only Theatre of Pain*, set the template for American-style GOTHIC ROCK, adding to British POST-PUNK's bass heavy death disco a bravado and blasphemy, spoken word and a wash of spooky guitars and keyboards. Did I mention blasphemy? Everything about Christian Death seemed designed to piss off the Catholic Church, from the name itself to lyrics about necrophilia, perversion and drugs, not to mention their "Litanies of Satan." The prime line-up consisted of Williams, guitarist VALOR KAND, keyboardist GITANE DEMONE and drummer David Glass. In 1985, Williams quit the underground rock star life for pursuit of more surrealist and experimental art musings and Kand took over the mic and the name. (Rozz later decided he wanted it back and then there were competing, confusing Christian Deaths on the market.) The resulting split caused a deep rift in the Goth time-space continuum: you were either Team Rozz or Team Valor. Until April 1, 1998, when Williams took his own life, by hanging. Then it hardly seemed to matter. What remains is a catalogue of boundary pushing, deeply macabre music from all parties that is required listening for anyone who wants to understand how it all began.

CHURCH OF SATAN Religion founded in 1968 by Anton Szander LaVey (1930–1997) in San Francisco, having very little to do with Christian, Jewish or Muslim concepts of Satan at all. Rather, it rejects heaven and hell and prayer in favour of individual responsibility, indulgence and the occasional Black Mass featuring a hot naked woman on an altar. Membership details are shadowy, but few Goths actually belong to the CoS (although MARILYN MANSON has) even if they like to wear inverted pentagrams and quote from the Satanic Bible. LaVey's daughter Karla ("The High Priestess of Hell"!) keeps the fires burning with her own First Satanic Church, a radio show and the occasional special appearance at HALLOWEEN club events near you.

CINNABON Chain of fast food kiosks serving cinnamon rolls and other gooey deserts, generally found in malls across America. Fictional place of employment for AZRAEL ABYSS of *Saturday Night Live*'s sketch GOTH TALK, meant to poke fun at how a dark prince has to work a MUNDANE low-wage food court job. *Circe: "Azrael, how does the evening find you?" Azrael: "Forlorn. I had to work a double shift at Cinnabon today."*

CLAN OF XYMOX Dutch SYNTHPOP band founded by guitarist/vocalist Ronny Moorings in 1981, originally known as Xymox. Part of the early wave of bands on 4AD Records practicing ethereal electronic alchemy with female vocalists (in their case, bassist Anke Wolbert); signed to PolyGram with negligible effect, later got a harder edge and hookup with METROPOLIS RECORDS. Remembered today mostly as the band with a name that starts with X. (Not to be confused with

X-Mal Deutschland.) Club hits include "Obsession" and "Imagination."

CLEOPATRA RECORDS American independent record company founded by Brian Perera in 1992 in California, specializing in Goth and INDUSTRIAL music. Best known for tributes and other compilation albums, but also nurtured many up-and-coming artists, notably SWITCHBLADE SYMPHONY and Mephisto Walz, as well as resurrecting out-of-print punk and metal classics on various sub imprints. Apart from the beloved *Goth Box* CD and DVD set, many of the comps were novelty and have not aged well, but for about ten years, a deal on Cleopatra was about as good as it got for a Goth band in North America. Current roster includes Finnish vamp rockers 69 Eyes.

CLOAK Sleeveless outerwear garment fastening at the neck, worn by both men and women. Many uses: for going to the opera, for playing MEDIEVAL fantasy games, and for dressing up like Count DRACULA. Cloaks have been associated with VAMPIRES since BELA LUGOSI wore one in the classic horror film, so you know Goths have followed suit.

CLOVES Type of cigarette blending tobacco and dried clove buds that emits a sweet smell and a crackling sound when lit. For some reason, a fashionable thing for Goths to smoke. In 2009, the government of the United States enacted a ban on cloves in a bid to inhibit cigarettes with a "characterizing flavour" from attracting children. Goths wept.

COCTEAU TWINS Scottish DREAMPOP band formed in 1979 by guitarist Robin Guthrie and bassist Will Heggie, known for the heavenly vocals of frontwoman Elizabeth Fraser. Showcased a minimal drum (machine) 'n' bass driven sound on 1982 debut *Garlands* (after which Heggie was replaced by Simon Raymonde); moved towards the dreamiest of pop, with layers of effects-laden guitars and Fraser's otherworldly singing of nonsense lyrics at the forefront. Defined the swirling, shoegazing sound and style of their label 4AD, until relationships between the parties soured; signing to major Capitol brought 1988's *Blue Bell Knoll* to more North American ears, with 1990's excessively produced *Heaven or Las Vegas* completing their transformation into a commercial entity, complete with radio singles and (gasp!) discernable lyrics. Behind the scenes, romantic ties between Guthrie and Fraser were on the brink, and the band collapsed during recording in 1997. A planned reunion at Coachella festival in 2005 was called off by Fraser. The Cocteaus remain ground zero for the ETHEREAL subgenre, and forerunners of such later day acts as Iceland's Sigur Ros. Most importantly, the Cocteaus gave ROMANTIGOTHS a soundtrack for clubbing. If you've ever watched someone on the dance floor who appears to be sweeping cobwebs from the air in slow motion and mouthing the words to some alien language, that's a Cocteau

Twins song playing, probably "Carolyn's Fingers" or "Iceblink Luck."

COFFIN A box to bury the dead, meant to be used just the once, and only after we've passed on. But Goths see no need to wait. While few have invested in actual coffins for their homes, coffin-shaped furniture is a popular choice, from expensive custom casket couches or bookshelves to more novelty-type items such as wine boxes or pillows.

COFFIN CARS A coffin modified to operate as a vehicle. Why would anyone bother? Because THE MUNSTERS had one called DRAG-U-LA, and it was quite cool. A fun weekend project for GOTHABILLY hobbyists.

COLDWAVE I. Musical movement born in France and Belgium in the late 1970s around experiments with POST-PUNK and electronics, a legit subgenre that's not necessarily Goth. 2. New wave of twenty-first century indie bands who wear black and like JOY DIVISION and early CURE records but would never deign to call themselves Goth. (Ed. note: POSEURS.) *See also: Darkwave*

COLLINS, ANDREW British journalist and TV screenwriter (b. March 4, 1965) who penned the hilarious "Bluffer's Guide to Goth" for *NME* in 1991, which remains the most spot-on answer to "What is Goth?" this author has yet to find, probably because Collins is a) an actual Goth, and b) a comedy writer. Went on to work for *Q, Select* and the BBC and to publish several memoirs of his misadventures and a biography of activist singer/songwriter Billy Bragg. Collins on why Goths buy skull-shaped candles: "Well, electric light is so *artificial*, isn't it? And light. And not shaped like a skull."

COLUMBINE Location outside Littleton, Colorado, site of a high school massacre April 20, 1999, in which two disgruntled students, Eric Harris and Dylan Klebold, shot and killed twelve students and one teacher, injuring dozens more and inadvertently causing a moral panic about violence and Gothdom. In the wake of the tragedy, in which the gunmen killed themselves, struggles to understand why led media to jump on the boys' appearance (black trench coats), habits (video gaming) and musical tastes (KMFDM), labeling them Goth even though they were most definitely not. They were also not MARILYN MANSON fans or members of the so-called TRENCHCOAT MAFIA clique at their school but that didn't stop media from vilifying those things too. Initial reports that the murderers were lashing out against bullying jocks had some Goths expressing sympathy or support for the misfits' cause, but most were as shocked and horrified as anyone. When tabloid TV and newspapers started declaring Goth a violent subculture (even Diane Sawyer on *20/20* pointed fingers at this "dark, underground national phenomenon") and some schools banned all-black clothing and trenchcoats in fear, Goth backlash was in full effect. Marilyn Manson took the brunt of it, while most kids just tried to stay out of the crossfire. To this day, violent acts committed by a teenager in black clothing can result in cheap knee-jerk reporting and a collective sigh from Goths everywhere.

COMBAT BOOTS Military boots designed for soldiers in combat but adopted by punks and Goths of both genders, particularly the RIVETHEAD crowd who enjoy their supreme stompiness factor. The old insult "Your mother wears combat boots" doesn't really work on us.

COMBICHRIST American-based "aggrotech" project started in 2003 by Norwegian vocalist/guitarist/ electronic music programmer Andy LaPlegua of Icon of Coil. Essentially a one-man band, he takes all the hallmarks of INDUSTRIAL EBM music and gives them a gothier makeover: more TATTOOS, more and spikier hair and more evil lyrics to go with the club-ready 4/4 stomp, a combo LaPlegua has dubbed "Techno Body Music." Breakout single "Get Your Body Beat" was released on June 6, 2006 (6/6/6, get it?), and spent six weeks on the Billboard charts. Oooh, scary! A prime example of Goth's special brand of self-deprecating black humour; to wit: some of the cheekiest album titles around, including *Sex, Drogen und Industrial* and *What the Fuck Is Wrong with You People?*

CONSTANTINE, STORM British author (b. 1956) of sci-fi and fantasy heaving with magic and sexuality. Her imaginative Wraeththu trilogy features post-apocalyptic hermaphrodites. That's not particularly Goth, but Storm is in her real life. She's even parlayed her expertise on the nephilim, those Biblical giants, into writing the liner notes for *Revelations* by the FIELDS OF THE NEPHILIM, those giants of GOTHIC ROCK.

CONVERGENCE Gathering of the denizens of the ALT. GOTHIC newsgroup, held annually in rotating host cities since 1995 and often referred to simply by the letter C plus the number of years running (e.g., C4 was held in Toronto). The volunteer-run event, now primarily organized through LiveJournal, provides an opportunity for net friends to meet in person and features the usual elements of a Goth festival (live bands, DJs, fashion shows, group outings, etc.). Blossomed into a full-fledged weekend event attracting the masses for a while, but it's really meant to serve its own specific community and, after some controversy about its growth (i.e., "Who are all these people we didn't invite?"), has scaled back to a more intimate meet-up. In 2006 in Seattle, they got to enjoy a surprise appearance from PETER MURPHY.

COOPER, ALICE American heavy metal singer (né Vincent Furnier, b. February 4, 1948) who set the bar for horrific GRAND GUIGNOL shock theatrics in a rock show in the late 1960s, using faked electrocutions, guillotine beheadings, dead babies, boa constrictor snakes and blood to great effect. Target of controversy, spinner of yarns, Cooper's long-standing myths include that he took his stage name from a seventeenth-century witch who contacted him through a Ouija board. Notable from his five-decade long career is his 1975 album *Welcome to My Nightmare*, with special guest VINCENT PRICE. Despite all this, Cooper has never been on most Goth playlists, perhaps because his music's actually pretty upbeat, and he's a born-again Christian golf nut.

CORBEAU A French Goth (literally "raven"). Prefer Gothique.

CORBIJN, ANTON Dutch photographer and filmmaker (b. May 20, 1955), modern master of the black-and-white image, most beloved for establishing the look of JOY DIVISION. He relocated from his homeland to ENGLAND specifically to meet and photograph the band in the 1970s, directed the video "Atmosphere" after the death of singer IAN CURTIS, and ultimately made the 2007 Curtis biopic *Control*. You don't see a black-and-white feature film about an underground band winning prizes at Cannes everyday. Dank u, Corbijn.

CORP GOTH Short for Corporate Goth, a term for a Goth with a professional job. Commonly used as an adjective to describe clothing suitable for office dress codes that won't make you gag. Websites and message boards help guide the Corp Goth to balance their day/night lives, answering such questions as "Can I wear my lip ring to the interview?" and reassuring folks that one isn't a POSEUR just for accepting employment that doesn't appreciate blue hair. If you spot a girl with a long velvet skirt and SILVER jewelry on your morning commute or a boy in your office prone to pinstriped suits, you're probably looking at a Corp Goth.

CORPSEPAINT Black and white face make-up as applied by black metal bands and their fans. Generally haphazard, with white all over the face and black EYELINER around the eyes and mouth, although sometimes more elaborate designs are created. In general, meant to look brutal and evil and not to be confused with Goth make-up styles, which are meant to look beautiful, albeit ghastly. Some similarities with CROW MAKE-UP, but neither can be recommended.

CORSET Garment designed to restrict and/or shape the torso, originally an undergarment now brazenly worn on its own by Goth girls of pretty much every size and stripe who can afford one. Constructed of a variety of materials, including silks, VELVETS, leather, LATEX or PVC, and with metal or plastic replacing the traditional whale boning, they are mass produced and available at lingerie and sex shops for cheap, but generally are best when custom made. Meant to be laced very tightly, resulting in an exaggerated silhouette and much cleavage, although few Goths practice actual body modification through corsetry. Rather, it is considered a staple of both formal and fetish wear. Every few years some pop star popularizes corsets as outerwear, but Goths get away with doing it all the time.

COSPLAY Short for costume play, an activity in which participants dress and act as a fictional character, commonly from Japanese anime or manga, or Western sci-fi or comics, often to attend fan conventions and pose for photographs. Since some of these characters can be "gothy," one may find a non-Goth person dressed in what would seem to outsiders to be Goth attire. A bad wig in a bright colour is the first giveaway you're dealing with cosplay.

COTHRON, KYNT Reality TV star of *The Amazing Race* season 12. Goth. *See also: Fiala, Vyxsin*

COUNT CHOCULA Fictional mascot for breakfast cereal of the same name introduced by General Mills in 1971, a spoof of BELA LUGOSI's Count DRACULA, sporting a brown-and-white tuxedo and cloak with monofang. Part of a gang of monster cereals also including Franken Berry and Boo Berry, the product features chocolate skull and BAT-shaped marshmallows and tons of sugar, with the side effect of turning your milk to chocolate milk. Part of a balanced Goth breakfast.

CRADLE OF FILTH British black/gothic/symphonic/ black symphonic gothic metal band, formed in Suffolk by Dani Filth in 1991. The sound of a HAMMER HORROR film as re-imagined as an extreme metal musical, CoF have too many GOTH POINTS to count: concept albums based on VAMPIRES, COUNTESS BÁTHORY or the stories of CLIVE BARKER; cameos by scream queen Ingrid Pitt and PINHEAD Doug Bradley; copious use of nudity and gore in art and performance; SISTERS OF MERCY covers; black leather, PVC and other shiny fetish outfits; and Dani's cheeky sense of black humour. So why aren't they Goth? Because they're heavy metal.

CRAMPS, THE American garage rock band, formed in New York in 1976 by kooky power couple Lux Interior (vocals) and Poison Ivy (guitar). Originators of the GOTHABILLY sound and style, combining American blues, R&B, surf and punk rock with B-movie monsters and junk pop culture into a sexed-up, swampy cocktail of swagger and spook. With rotating membership and record company woes, they never broke through to the mainstream, but they sure knew how to write a pop hit: "Human Fly," "Garbageman," "Goo Goo Muck" and "Can Your Pussy Do the Dog?" to name just a few. They did get a song ("Surfin' Dead") onto the soundtrack of *The Return of the Living Dead* in 1985 and crashed onto network TV for *Beverly Hills 90210*'s 1995 HALLOWEEN episode. And damn if they didn't look cool doing it: Lux's black PVC pants painted on, Poison Ivy's flame hair and go-go boots. The band's end came suddenly on February 4, 2009, when Interior died of aortic dissection. Perhaps The Cramps were too much fun for some Goths, but the world is a lot less interesting without them in it. R.I.P.

CREATURES, THE Musical side-project for singer SIOUXSIE SIOUX and drummer Budgie, of British superstars SIOUXSIE AND THE BANSHEES, formed in 1981. By 1991, the two had married; by 1997 The Banshees were dead and The Creatures became the duo's priority, but by 2007 the couple was divorced and the musical collaborations had come to an end. Despite several critically acclaimed albums, some cheeky covers (Mel Tormé's "Right Now," The Troggs' "Wild Thing") and the pedigree of its members, The Creatures are often forgotten.

CREEPERS Men's shoe with thick corrugated-like soles and pointed toe and uppers of leather or suede often in a two-tone black/white or leopard print, more accurately known as a "Brothel creeper." Originally popularized in ENGLAND in the 1950s, taken up by the punks in the 1970s, adopted by Goths in the 1980s and now seen primarily on PSYCHOBILLIES and other cool retro cats. Well-known manufacturers include Underground (traditional, unisex styles) and T.U.K. (branching out to girlie creepers and creeper/sneaker hybrids).

CREEPY CUTE Something a little bit scary, a little bit soft and cuddly. Think crocheted ZOMBIE dolls. The idea started in Japan. Of course.

CRIMPER Hair styling tool used to wave or "crimp" hair in a jagged pattern by pressing it between two heated sawtooth-shaped plates. Legend has it the crimper was invented in 1972 to style Barbra Streisand. This didn't stop it from becoming widespread in the counterculture throughout the 1980s. Goths are some of the only folks who still own crimpers today, if only for the few times a year they try to make their hair look like ROBERT SMITH's.

CRIMSON GHOST 1. Skull logo used by horror punkers THE MISFITS, so named for the 1940s TV serial whose poster inspired the creepy black-and-white image. First used on 1979 single "Horror Business" and appearing on Misfits' releases and merch (plus plenty of fan TATTOOS) ever since. It's kind of like the Goth equivalent of a picture of Che: kids wear it to look cool even if they have no idea what it is. 2. Song on the 1997 Misfits album *American Psycho*. 3. A number of horror punk bands who would be obvious Misfits rip-offs even if they weren't named after their favourite group's logo.

CROW, THE Comic created by American James O'Barr, originally published in 1989 by Caliber Comics, about protagonist Eric DRAVEN, a victim of a random attacker who kills his fiancée and leaves him for dead until he is resurrected by a supernatural crow. Using newfound special powers, Eric sets out to systematically kill those responsible. The story of pain, love lost and revenge hit a chord, and was made into a feature film in 1994 starring Brandon Lee. Tragedy struck the set and Lee was killed during filming. There are many reasons Goths love *The Crow*: O'Barr allegedly based Eric's character on IAN CURTIS, PETER MURPHY and IGGY POP; the soundtrack for the movie included a new song, "Burn," by THE CURE and a cover of JOY DIVISION's "Dead Souls" by NINE INCH NAILS. Also, Eric's costume for the film — tight black leather pants, trenchcoat, make-up — has been resurrected countless times by Goth Boys whether they've read the comic or not.

CROW MAKE-UP Style of make-up featured in the 1994 movie *THE CROW*, in which star Brandon Lee as Eric DRAVEN puts on white face with black eyes modeled after a masquerade mask. An easy HALLOWEEN costume that suffers from overuse. Frankly, as the GOTHIC CHARM SCHOOL guide suggests, friends don't let friends dress like the Crow.

CRÜXSHADOWS, THE American SYNTHPOP band formed in Jacksonville, Florida, in 1992 by lead singer Rogue, he of the CYBERLOX hair and suspicious British accent. Frankly, quite a curious beast: cyber/fetish aesthetic, mythological lyrics, perky dance beats, *NSync-style headsets, violin player, the motto of "Live Love Be Believe." Could it be true they are consciously satirizing Goth itself? How then to explain the earnestness? To their credit, have managed more than a dozen releases independently, cracked Billboard dance singles charts and developed an ever-growing global fanbase, particularly in GERMANY. But despite appearances, there's something not quite Goth about them. The fact that they eagerly identify themselves as Goth might be the first clue.

CULT, THE British rock band formed in 1983 by singer IAN ASTBURY and guitarist Billy Duffy by altering the name of their previous band, Death Cult, in order to sound less Goth. They hadn't really been Goth since the original Astbury project, the POST-PUNKY Southern Death Cult (1981–1983), but therein lies one of the many paradoxes of this outfit: they've always been more of a psychedelic rock band, a heavy metal band, a stadium rock band, and yet . . . Goth icons. Blame it on the 1984 debut *Dreamtime*, a sonic ritual of shamanism and shoegazing before there was a name for that. Or 1985's breakthrough opus *Love*, with its seductive hit singles "She Sells Sanctuary" and "Rain." Not even 1987's rock reinvention *Electric* could strip them of their GOTH CARDS. Okay, perhaps their oldest U.K. fans had had enough of the AC/DC riffs and bloated rock star antics (not to mention touring with Guns N' Roses and Aerosmith) by the time that the U.S. chart-topper *Sonic Temple* came in 1988. But some of us held out all the way to the dreadful *Ceremony* record in 1991. A series of member changes, hiatuses, hits compilations and unremarkable reunions has plagued the band since, but damn if it wasn't great to hear the *Love* album in its entirety on the 2009 tour.

CURE, THE British alternative rock/GOTHIC ROCK/ NEW WAVE/POST-PUNK band formed in 1978 by singer/ guitarist ROBERT SMITH, drummer Lol Tolhurst and bassist Michael Dempsey, who went through a "Goth phase" from 1980–1982. Rather, that's what Wikipedia has to say about The Cure, in what could surely be called one of the online encyclopedia's great fails. The Cure, more than any other popular music group, has never had a "Goth phase." Rather, since its introductory single "Killing an Arab" (which has done more to keep Albert Camus' *The Stranger*, upon which it was based, on the bookshelves of young people than most universities), The Cure has epitomized Goth in all its forms, defining it, transforming it. While it can certainly said that the band's early triptych of melancholy — *Seventeen Seconds* (1980), *Faith* (1981) and *Pornography* (1983) — with their stark, bass-heavy rhythms and nihilistic worldview, are the most typically Goth, there is as much romancing of death throughout its catalogue. Well, except for when they're happy: "The Lovecats" and "Let's Go to Bed" may have been the start of PERKY GOTH. For three decades, Robert Smith and various mates (arguably, none nearly as important as the singer himself) have continued to lead the Goth nation, with new music and epic live shows. *See also: Disintegration*

CURIOSA Concert tour organized by ROBERT SMITH in 2004, headlined by THE CURE and featuring POST-PUNK revivalists INTERPOL and The Rapture as well as noisemakers Mogwai and Muse. Played twenty shows in very un-Goth–like amphitheatres across North America.

CURTIS, IAN British singer (1956–1980), lead voice of POST-PUNK pioneers JOY DIVISION, a romantic poet for the age of alienation. Curtis was known for his unique performance style, dancing frantically not unlike a man caught in an epileptic seizure, which he also suffered from. Committed suicide by hanging on May 18, 1980, just before the band's first North American tour, which some may say makes for many GOTH POINTS but I say just makes for much sadness. *Control*, a film about his life based on the book *Touching from a Distance* (by his widow Deborah), was released in 2007. Buried at Macclesfield Cemetery in Cheshire, ENGLAND, beneath a stone bearing the title of his best-known work, Love Will Tear Us Apart.

CUSHING, PETER British actor (1913–1994) best known for his roles in HAMMER HORROR films, most notably as Victor Frankenstein in 1957's *The Curse of Frankenstein* and Van Helsing in 1958's *Horror of Dracula*. Vegetarian, bird-watcher and best friend to iconic on-screen DRACULA Christopher Lee, Cushing never particularly embraced the dark side, nor reached the level of sainthood of his pal VINCENT PRICE, yet he remains a grand duke of Gothdom. Died of prostate cancer; the whereabouts of his cremated remains are unknown.

CUTTING The act of intentionally cutting one's own skin, usually the wrist or forearm, clinically referred as "self-harm." Those who do it are called cutters, and they are not necessarily suicidal. A 2006 study of teenagers by Glasgow researchers found the practice more prevalent in those who identify as Goth, and anecdotal evidence suggests that to be true, leading to renewed media panic about the "dangers" of Gothdom. However, the practice seems to have become a somewhat socially acceptable act (or at least the displaying of scars and talking about it is), only since the emergence of EMO in the 2000s. (The crass but popular expression "remember, EMO kids, down the road, not across the street" makes a joke of the cutting of wrists for attention, since sideways is not an effective way to cause fatal bleeding.) Therefore, without making light of a serious and distressing psychological condition, I'm going to say there is nothing intrinsically Goth about cutting, and the word is listed here only to refute the stereotype.

CYBERDOG British clothing company founded by Terry Davy and Spiros Vlahos in 1994, which defined the CYBERGOTH look and helped launch it into the mainstream. The clothing is meant for clubbing and features reflective stripes, secret pockets, bright neon colours, shiny material like PVC and at times even real electronics synching the graphics on a shirt to music's BPM. Likewise, their retail shops (starting with the original stall in CAMDEN) have featured bouncy dance floors, loud techno music and perky staff ready to suit you up for a night out. How inspired are they by sci-fi and futurism? They claim their mascot dog Chichi was actually abducted by aliens and taken into outer space, where he gets all their great design ideas and brings them back to Earth. The future of fashion — today!

CYBERGOTH Contemporary offshoot of Goth emerging at the turn of the millennium from out of the cyberpunk and rave scene, concerned with futurism in fashion, FUTUREPOP in music and flauting conventions of all-black attire and sourpuss faces. Rather, Cybergoths typically dress in shiny, bright neon colours, super high platform boots, outrageous synthetic hair extensions, GOGGLES and other exaggerated accessories ripped from anime or sci-fi, listen to electronic music and generally spend more time in clubs than CEMETERIES. And while some TRAD GOTHS find little in common with these club kids and their musical preferences, they have injected the scene with much creativity and taken it into new, exciting directions.

CYBERLOX Artificial hair extension material made of ribbon sewn into a tube shape, also referred to as "tubular crin." Stretchy and light, it is available in a variety of colours and sizes and is commonly sewn into hair FALLS, sometimes with metallic pieces, yarn or foam for temporary accessorizing. If the person dancing next to you has hair that looks like it's straight out of a gothic sci-fi anime comic, it's probably cyber-lox. *See also: Synthdreads*

DEATHHAWK

DAMNED, THE British punk band formed in 1976 by singer DAVE VANIAN, bassist Captain Sensible and drummer Rat Scabies. Definitely predated Goth (they are credited with releasing the first punk recording with the single "New Rose") but did much to put the idea out there of incorporating the macabre: Vanian dressed like a gentleman VAMPIRE and they wrote songs about horror movies, for example. But unlike a lot of the BATCAVERS to follow, The Damned were always fun. Their parody of the Beatles' *White Album* with their *Black Album* cover was fun. The whole 1985 ÜBERGOTH major label breakthrough album *Phantasmagoria* was fun ("Grimly Fiendish!"). Heck, Captain Sensible's biggest solo hit was called "Happy Talk." Not so fun: the band's repeated splits and hiatuses. Things seem to be back on track: 2008's *So, Who's Paranoid?*, featuring the single "Little Miss Disaster," was cross-promoted with EMILY THE STRANGE. Fun.

DANCING FERRET Concert production company in Philadelphia founded by DJ Ferret (Patrick Rodgers) in 1995, runs the city's oldest weekly Goth club night, Nocturne, and produces the annual DRACULA'S BALL. From 1998 to 2008, also operated Dancing Ferret Discs, an independent record label releasing GOTHIC ROCK, INDUSTRIAL and SYNTHPOP music, most notably the majority of THE CRÜXSHADOWS' catalogue.

DANDY A male preoccupied with sartorial elegance. BYRON was one; BAUDELAIRE too. Many STEAMPUNK and ROMANTIGOTH men could be considered modern dandies, concerned as they are with dressing sharp, acting proper and enjoying language and leisure. A tip of the fancy hat to them.

DANZIG, GLENN American singer (né Glenn Allen Anzalone, b. June 23, 1955) founder of THE MISFITS, SAMHAIN and Danzig, lover of B-movies and Black Sabbath, sometimes called "Black Elvis." A true HORROR PUNK and heavy metal icon, but about %666 too macho to be truly considered Goth. Don't tell him I said that: he could crush us all.

DARK AMBIENT Subgenre of AMBIENT electronic music originating in the 1970s that included many early INDUSTRIAL acts and is sometimes used interchangeably with ETHEREAL or DARKWAVE, but has become more connected to the metal scene than the Goth scene.

DARK CABARET Revival of cabaret and burlesque theatrics mixed with a more punk or Goth musical styling, most often applied to THE DRESDEN DOLLS. Popularized by the 2005 compilation *Projekt Presents: A Dark Cabaret*.

DARK FAIRY *See: Fairiegoth*

DARKRAVE Monthly DJ night held in Toronto since 1999, organized by DJ Lazarus. Bringing together

INDUSTRIAL, EBM, SYNTHPOP, psytrance and other dark electronic genres and the day-glo backpack—carrying fans who love them, probably directly responsible for introducing the CYBERGOTH scene to Toronto. (Themes like "pirates vs. ninjas" encouraging creative costuming.) Any reference to the event as "dorkrave" by TRAD GOTHS in the area is mostly in jest. Mostly.

DARK REALMS American magazine published from 2000 to 2008, exploring the "shadows of art, music and culture." Edited by Mr. Dark with art direction by Christine Filipak and featuring covers by dark fantasy artist Joseph Vargo.

DARK SHADOWS American television's first and only Gothic soap opera, created by Dan Curtis and airing from 1966 to 1971. Gothic as in fog-drenched mansions, mad heroines, ghosts — and an alluring gentleman VAMPIRE named Barnabas Collins the likes of which pop culture had not yet seen. Syndication and cult status followed, but it wasn't until TIM BURTON announced he was making a new feature starring JOHNNY DEPP as Barnabas that most modern Goths truly took notice.

DARK SIDE OF THE NET Online database of links to Gothic and horror websites, curated by Carrie Carolin from 1993 to 2010. Carrie now maintains Darklinks, a blog and Twitter account focused on news.

DARKWAVE 1. Musical subgenre emerging from Europe in the 1980s and applied in the 1990s to new Goth bands with more NEW WAVE or AMBIENT tendencies, as opposed to rock 'n' roll or INDUSTRIAL, also referred to as ETHEREAL. The North American darkwave scene was particularly promoted by New York label PROJEKT RECORDS, which used the term in its mail-order catalogue. 2. Montreal's longest-running alternative/Goth/NEW WAVE music DJ night, currently held at the Club Sapphir. *See also: Coldwave*

DEAD CAN DANCE Australian-British group founded in 1981 by singers/multi-instrumentalists LISA GERRARD and Brendan Perry. To POST-PUNK they added folk musics from around the globe and across the ages, creating a unique kind of exotic, hypnotic neoclassical hybrid perfect for REN FAIRS, ROMANTIGOTH fashion shows and general swooning. But it was the haunting ying/yang of their vocals that truly made DCD ETHEREAL icons. They split in 1998 but several excellent compilations exist for those who missed them the first time around: key tracks include Perry's "The Ubiquitous Mr. Lovegrove" and Gerrard's "Yulunga (Spirit Dance)." BAUHAUS exquisitely covered their "Severance" on a 2005 reunion tour.

DEATH Fictional character in the comic book series *The Sandman*, created by NEIL GAIMAN and Mike Dringenberg. A personification of Death itself in the guise of a pretty, perky, PALE girl in black jeans and a

T-shirt, with black hair, black EYELINER swirls on her face and an ANKH pendant around her neck, it's no wonder all the Goth Girls love her.

DEATH GUILD Club night in San Francisco billed as the longest-running weekly Goth/INDUSTRIAL DJ night in the U.S., launched by DJ Decay in 1992.

DEATHHAWK Goth version of a Mohawk hairdo, favoured by death rockers of both genders. As with the Mohawk, sides of the head are shaved or clipped super short, with a band of length left in the middle and forced upwards. Rather than sharply defined, heavily gelled spikes, the deathhawk is more of a tangled, teased mess. Techniques for putting it up involve CRIMPING, BACKCOMBING and loads of hairspray. Famous death-hawk wearers are Jonny Slut from SPECIMEN and model RAZOR CANDI.

DEATH ROCK Musical subgenre that came after punk but before GOTHIC ROCK, sprung from Los Angeles around 1979, not unlike London's BATCAVE scene. (Although the two wouldn't know about each other 'til later.) It mixed the raw and aggressive energy of punk with spooky synths and horror tropes, but took itself way more seriously than the similar sounding HORROR PUNKS, as epitomized by its key band, the blasphemous art project CHRISTIAN DEATH. The term fell out of fashion in the 1980 and 1990s, but Cyber backlash inspired a revival, with new bands eager to explore the old-school sound and dedicated websites like deathrock.com and deathrock.org providing the guidance. Some use this term interchangeably with Gothic rock but it has little in common with THE SISTERS set.

DEETZ, LYDIA Fictional character in TIM BURTON's horror-comedy *Beetlejuice* (1988), a teenage Goth Girl played by a young and wide-eyed Winona Ryder. One of the best loved depictions of modern Goths in all of cinema: the self-described "strange and unusual" Deetz dresses all in black, practises photography and is the only one in her family who can see the ghosts haunting their home. A whole generation fell in love with Ryder after this, enough even to forgive her years later for nearly ruining Francis Ford Coppola's *DRACULA* film with her laughably fake British accent.

DEMASK Fashion designers specializing in high-end LATEX and leather wear, of the kind often seen on the cover of *Bizarre* magazine or at the fanciest of fetish balls. Founded in 1990 and operating retail shops in Amsterdam, Munich and Dortmund. (NYC's East Village shop, R.I.P.) You need the perfect neck CORSET, BATWING leather CLOAK or pair of RUBBER pants that attach your penis directly to a full rubber hood worn by your partner? Demask has you covered, literally.

DEMONE, GITANE American singer, musician and performance artist, best known as a vocalist/keyboardist for L.A. DEATH ROCK icons CHRISTIAN DEATH from

1983 to 1989. Her provocative interpretations of sex and surrealism have continued in a variety of musical and visual art experiments, but she will probably forever be remembered for the cover to her 1993 solo EP *Lullabies for a Troubled World*, on which she is shown blindfolded and pointing a gun at her own mouth.

DEMONIA Footwear company responsible for about %90 of those big honking platform BUCKLE BOOTS seen on Goth girls and boys, as well as CREEPERS, MARY JANES, sneakers, stilettos, WINKLE PICKERS for the Trads and literally hundreds of other styles of a somewhat extreme or alternative nature. (Also: sandals with skulls.) Part of the company Pleasure USA, "the world's largest supplier of sexy shoes." What's really sexy is their budget price point, although that doesn't make you feel any better when they start falling apart. Still, towering over the competition.

DENNY'S Family restaurant chain that never closes, popular in America as an after-hours hang-out for Goth kids who need a place to stay up all night drinking coffee. Generally attracts a pretty low-rent crowd in the evenings so Goths can blend in, but getting hassled in or kicked out of a Denny's is a sort of rite of passage too.

DEPP, JOHNNY American actor (b. June 9, 1963), granted honourary Goth status for his gothy starring roles in TIM BURTON's films *EDWARD SCISSORHANDS*,

Sleepy Hollow, *Sweeney Todd* and DARK SHADOWS. Because even Goths need someone whose pin-up they can put in their lockers.

DEPRESSION The one stereotype about Goths that's got to go: we're no more or less depressed than any other segment of the population. Wearing mourning colours, writing despairing poetry and celebrating sadness through ridiculous interpretive dance is not the same thing as suffering from a mood disorder.

DEV, THE London pub Devonshire Arms, located near CAMDEN MARKET, long a second home for Goth/RIVETHEAD types fancying a SNAKEBITE, horror-themed décor and the company of other dark souls. Or it was until 2007, when it was bought out and rebranded HobGoblin, more of a rock/metal bar, and its one-time strict GOTH DRESS CODE posted at the door was relaxed to simply "No Wankers." While many regulars have boycotted the new joint, others still find it a decent place for a pre-concert meet-up. However, it seems long gone are the days when the bartender would draw a skull and crossbones into the foam of your Guinness.

DEVIANTART Online community for user-generated artwork launched in 2000 and boasting more than 14 million members. A popular place for young Goth artists and photographers to upload and share their work; heavy on fantasy and anime type stuff.

DEVILOCK Hairstyle associated with HORROR PUNKS, as popularized by Jerry Only of THE MISFITS, in which the back and sides are kept short but the bangs are worn long and slicked down over the middle of the face into a hard, exaggerated point. Mostly a guy thing. Also, a song by The Misfits from their 1983 album *Earth A.D.*

DIGITALIS, RAVEN American writer, DJ, photographer and Neopagan priest (né Colin Smith, b. July 29, 1983) based in Missoula, Montana. Author of *Goth Craft: The Magickal Side of Dark Culture*, which shed a light on the areas where witchcraft and Goth converge.

DIRGE, ROMAN American writer and artist (b. April 29, 1972), creator of the comic book series *Lenore: The Cute Little Dead Girl*, based on the EDGAR ALLAN POE poem "Lenore." The heavily TATTOOED former magician has also worked in animation and recently developed his first video game, *Vampire Puff Puff*.

DISINTEGRATION Masterwork album by THE CURE, released May 1, 1989, whereupon it quickly became the band's greatest commercial success — double platinum in the U.S. with hit singles in "Lovesong," "Lullaby," "Pictures of You" and "Fascination Street." This is not why many critics, not to mention *South Park* character Kyle, have declared *Disintegration* "the best album ever!" It was the return to gloom for the band after a string of pop hits that, despite being the product of serious malaise in the life of twenty-nine-going-on-petrified singer

ROBERT SMITH, balanced deathly solemnity and the sound of loss and longing with lush orchestration and layers of heartfelt loveliness. Everyone who says this epic album is a total bummer with the exception of "Lovesong" clearly doesn't get the seductive appeal of ache and probably isn't Goth. Truly, a Desert Island Disc.

DR. MARTENS Boots of choice for skinheads, punks, grunge rock stars and working class types, affectionately known as Docs. Invented by an actual German doctor, Klaus Märtens. Introduced to the masses by English shoemakers in 1960 with the debut of the eight-hole cherry red model 1460. Docs are known for comfortable soles, bright yellow stitching and association with racist shithead shitkickers. So why would Goths wear 'em? Because some days you can't bear to put on the five-inch heels. Or you need plain footwear for a job interview that isn't a gross loafer. Maybe your entire wardrobe is stuck in the '80s. Sure, they're not really as "rebellious" as their marketing would like you to believe, but they really do go with anything, which is why there's probably a pair of black eight-hole Docs in every Goth's closet in the world. If you really need to ÜBER it up, there's always the eighteen-hole PVC model.

DOG COLLAR Why do some Goths wear an accessory made for dogs around their necks? Well, the punks started it. We adorn ourselves in collars (also called chokers) made of leather, lace, VELVET or steel, primarily as a fashion accessory but sometimes, for those in actual BDSM relationships, as a symbol of submission. Collars are often decorated with D-RINGS, to which a leash can be attached. In 2008 in ENGLAND, Goth Tasha Maltby was asked to get off a city bus because her collar/leash was considered some kind of safety hazard; after accusing the bus company of discrimination, she made news headlines worldwide for admitting to being the "human pet" of her fiancé Dani Graves. There was so much media coverage that a Google image search for "Goth" turns up her photo everytime, but certainly, not all Goths wear dog collars. *See also: Neck corset*

DOKTOR AVALANCHE Drummer for THE SISTERS OF MERCY. More accurately, the name given to a series of drum machines used by The Sisters instead of a live drummer, starting with a Boss DR55 "Dr. Rhythm" and including an Oberheim DMX (*First and Last and Always* era) and Akai S900 (*Floodland*) and eventually graduating into the digital realm. The good Doktor also answers emails on the Sisters website, although the snarkiness of his advice sure makes him sound a lot like bandleader ANDREW ELDRICH.

DOMINION 1. British music magazine launched October 2009 and published monthly as a supplement to metal mag *Terrorizer*. Editors boast that it's more than just a Goth zine, and they're right; it covers the entire dark alternative spectrum, from INDUSTRIAL and EBM to ye old DEATH ROCK and beyond, focusing on interviews and reviews. Essential reading to keep up with the European kids. 2. Song by THE SISTERS OF MERCY from the album *FLOODLAND*, released as a single in 1988 and also known as "Dominion/Mother Russia." A music video filmed in Jordan could be considered the original GOTHS IN HOT WEATHER. 3. Sisters of Mercy fan club mailing list. 4. Club night in Dublin, billed as Ireland's longest-running weekly Goth/Industrial night, featuring DJs, live music and music videos. Currently held in the Cellar of Murray's Bar. 5. Filipino Gothic metal band formed 1994.

DONOR A person in the so-called real VAMPIRE community who donates blood to a partner/loved one/interested party, who drinks it. About as common in Gothdom as spotting an actual vampire. *See also: Modern vampires*

DOOM COOKIE A derogatory term for a Goth POSEUR, someone who tries hard to look and act Goth but comes off like a walking cliché of overwrought poetry and misguided fashion choices with no understanding of the music or subculture. Why the general word poseur doesn't suffice here I'm not sure, other than that young Goths do have a way of amping up catty behaviour to the next level. *See also: Mall Goth*

DRAC-IN-A-BOX British clothing company launched by Carmilla and Dorian in 1999. Designs slant towards the Trad/ROMANTIGOTH side, with frilly VICTORIAN gowns, black bridal veils and pinstriped top coats, but online shop also stocks some Cyber. High quality, original stuff made by and for Goths. Bravo.

DRACULA I. Fictional VAMPIRE count from Transylvania created by author BRAM STOKER in the 1897 novel of the same name. The archetypal NOSFERATU — he gave the creatures so many of their attributes: sucking the blood of beautiful girls; hypnotic powers; shapeshifting into BATS, fog, wolves and the like; sleeping in a coffin full of dirt; lack of a reflection in mirrors; etc. etc. Both animalistic and aristocratic, he certainly had his way with the ladies, which may explain his enduring influence on pop culture today: in film, TV, books, games, toys, even breakfast cereal. A list of these adaptations could fill dozens of books and has. May I recommend *A Dracula Handbook* by Elizabeth Miller and *In Search of Dracula* by Raymond T. McNally and Radu Florescu? And may I also recommend that if you're going to dress up in a CAPE and FANGS for HALLOWEEN (or any other day), you read Stoker's original novel first? It's a classic for a reason. 2. Horror film directed by Tod Browning for Universal Studios in 1931, starring BELA LUGOSI as the Count, based on a stage play based on the book. Of the myriad versions of the tale, this black-and-white supernatural chiller is the one to watch.

DRACULA'S BALL VAMPIRE-themed party, held every three months in Philadelphia since 1999, featuring

DJs, live performances, vendors and costumed blood-sucker enthusiasts.

DRAG-U-LA 1. Coffin car prop made for the 1960s TV show *THE MUNSTERS*, in which a casket was tricked out with organ pipes, a tombstone and other gothy accessories to create a vehicle for Grandpa Munster to drag race with. 2. Song by ROB ZOMBIE from his 1998 album *Hellbilly Deluxe*.

DRAVEN 1. Eric Draven, fictional protagonist of James O'Barr's graphic novel *THE CROW*, portrayed by Brandon Lee in the 1994 film. 2. Draven Shoes, cheap sneakers worn by the occasional misguided MALL GOTH (likely fooled by the special-edition MISFITS high-tops), but best left to EMO skateboarders.

DREADS Dreadlocks, a style of matted hair traditionally worn by Rastafarians and Hindus for spiritual purposes, adopted by Goths as a fashion statement. The CYBERGOTHS started it with their synthetic dreads in bright colours and futuristic materials, popularizing the look of actual dreads in the community.

DREAMPOP Musical subgenre emerging from the U.K. in the mid to late 1980s, defined as "nebulous, distorted guitars with murmured vocals sometimes completely smudged into a wall of noise" by journalist Simon Reynolds in 1991 and as epitomized by 4AD acts as such as COCTEAU TWINS and This Mortal

Coil. Essentially, it's SHOEGAZER with more ETHEREAL female vocals.

DRESDEN DOLLS Boston DARK CABARET duo of AMANDA PALMER (vocals, piano) and Brian Viglione (drums, guitars) formed in 2000 after Brian spotted Amanda performing at a HALLOWEEN party. With their theatrical make-up and vaudevillian showmanship, the pair helped kickstart the DARK CABARET genre, scoring high-profile gigs with NINE INCH NAILS and Lollapalooza. Only two full-length albums so far, 2003's self-titled debut and 2006's *Yes, Virginia...*, and the band's future is uncertain but both are continuing to make much music so you won't run out of places to wear your striped tights anytime soon.

D-RING Piece of hardware, usually made of metal, in the shape of a D, affixed to an item such as clothing onto which you can attach or tie other items. A pretty universal way to Goth up any wardrobe, most often found on CORSETS, wrist cuffs, bracelets and boots as purely decorative but also standard issue for TRIPP BONDAGE PANT to attach extra straps.

DROP DEAD Festival for underground and independent music, with a focus on DEATH ROCK, BATCAVE, PSYCHOBILLY and other old-school genres. Started in New York City in 2002, migrating to Europe in 2007, where it is now held in a different country each year. A companion magazine emerged from NYC in

2005 for five issues before going digital and, shockingly, embracing new hipster music from outside Gothdom. Meanwhile, the festival remains a sanctuary for thousands of people with DEATHHAWKS who still love SEX GANG CHILDREN.

ELVIRA

EBAY Online auction site, where one can buy an endless supply of new and used clothing, accessories, music, books, movies and art of the Goth persuasion. Because not everyone has a HOT TOPIC at his/her local mall, or sometimes you really need to resell your entire WAX TRAX! vinyl collection to some lonely RIVETHEAD somewhere far away. Once a place for DIY designers and craftsfolk to start up their indie businesses, has now been usurped by ETSY.

EBM Short for Electronic Body Music, a subgenre of INDUSTRIAL music characterized by minimal, repetitive beats, clean production and vocalists who! shout! commands! Phrase coined by Ralf Hütter of German electronic music pioneers Kraftwerk in 1978 and popularized in mid to late 1980s to describe the early recordings of Front 242, DAF and Nitzer Ebb. EBM acted as a kind of connective tissue between GOTHIC ROCK and industrial clubs and communities, introducing a harder electronic sound (and more army boots) to dance floors in the years between NEW WAVE's demise and the rise of American industrial rock, although some TRAD GOTHS found the intrusion unacceptable. The mainstream/cross-over appeal of the originators (now referred to as "old school EBM") faded in the 1990s but a fresh influx of darker EBM bands such as Leaether Strip, :wumpscut: et al. found an audience all their own, perfectly timed for the emergence of CYBERGOTH. *See also: Futurepop*

ECHO AND THE BUNNYMEN British POST-PUNK band formed in Liverpool in 1978 by singer Ian McCulloch, guitarist Will Sergeant and bassist Les Pattinson; split in 1993 and reformed in 1996, active to present day. A kinder, gentler early Goth group, their songs were filled with melodrama and mystery but less mad bleakness than their contemporaries. Mainstream success came through placement in Hollywood movie soundtracks: "Bring on the Dancing Horses" for *Pretty in Pink* and their cover of The Doors' "People Are Strange" prominently heard in THE LOST BOYS. But it's their majestic ballad "The Killing Moon," from 1984's *Ocean Rain*, which has secured them a spot of honour as a slow dance soundtrack to every Goth wedding 'til the end of time.

EDWARD SCISSORHANDS Gothic fantasy film (1990), directed by TIM BURTON and starring JOHNNY DEPP as the titular Edward, a monstrous yet innocent creature with wild BACKCOMBED hair, PALE face, fetishy outfits and nasty looking scissors for hands. A dark fantasy retelling of FRANKENSTEIN (Edward's inventor is played by VINCENT PRICE) mixed with *Beauty and the Beast* (Edward's love interest is played by Winona Ryder), the film was a critical and box office success, establishing Depp as a modern Goth heartthrob. The Edward Scissorhands look is now iconic Goth Boy. Hence, perhaps second only to THE CROW as the one costume you really shouldn't wear to HALLOWEEN parties anymore if you don't want to show up dressed like twelve other people.

ELDER GOTH Simply put, an old Goth. More charitably, an older member of the Goth community who continues to dress up, listen to the music and actively participate in the scene to some extent. The term seems to have originated at the turn of the millennium, when the first wave of Goths hit their forties, although at precisely what age one becomes an "elder" varies from thirties through to fifties. While the term is used respectfully, it doesn't necessarily imply authority or wisdom or GOTHER THAN THOU—ness. It's just a nicer way of saying someone has been around the foggy block a few times. Most Elder Goths have embraced the term and use it without a whiff of irony; the Elder Goth cocktail hour was a popular event at CONVERGENCE gatherings. *Compare: Recovering Goth*

ELDRITCH, ANDREW British singer (né Andrew William Harvey Taylor, b. May 15, 1959) and, as leader of THE SISTERS OF MERCY, the Pope of Gothdom. As the old joke goes, when WAYNE HUSSEY (ex-Sisters) dies and goes to heaven, he finds Eldritch sitting on a throne and says to the Angel Gabriel, "I didn't know Andrew was dead," to which Gabriel replies, "No, that's God. He only thinks he's Andrew." One cannot exaggerate the prominence of Eldritch as figurehead, part of the

Trinity of Goth Frontmen alongside PETER MURPHY and ROBERT SMITH. Or his disgust at the thought of ever, ever, ever being considered a Goth, never mind leader of the pack. (In 1997, he threatened to cancel the Sisters' first North American appearance in seven years at the Dark Harvest Festival because some of the other acts on the bill were too Goth. The offending acts were removed and the band played on, while some audience members sported homemade "Too Goth for Andrew" buttons.) Still, while maddeningly arrogant, as the voice and brain of the most important band in the GOTHIC ROCK genre, he remains an intellectual and creative force. Even if, like some kind of Axl Rose, he keeps promising us new recordings that never come.

ELEGY French magazine of dark music and culture, published bimonthly since 1998. While heavy on band interviews and reviews, and packaged with a free sampler CD, *Elegy* also stands out for its coverage of the visual arts and photography, with striking covers. In 2006, expanded to a bilingual edition for the Spanish/Portuguese market.

ELVIRA Horror hostess character created by American actress/comedian Cassandra Peterson (b. September 17, 1951) in 1981 for a late-night TV show called *Movie Macabre*, where she found success screening B-grade horror flicks and cracking sassy, sexy jokes. With her low, low, low cut, cleavage-revealing black dress and high, high, high black beehive hairstyle, Elvira: Mistress of the Dark became the predominant stereotype of a modern-day vampress, as evidenced by the number of pre-packaged Elvira-style costumes for sale at Hallowen. Her empire has grown to include comic books, a pinball machine, dolls, and feature films, plus a 2007 reality TV show, *The Search for the Next Elvira*. Pro: having someone as talented and hilarious as Peterson represent Goth Girls is a Win! Con: having normal people shout "Hey, Elvira!" at every gothy girl whether one looks anything like her or not is an annoying curse. *See also: Morticia*

EMILY THE STRANGE Fictional character created by American skateboard clothing design company Cosmic Debris in the early 1990s. Emily wears the same black dress everyday, with striped tights and MARY JANE shoes and is often accompanied by her black cats. She has an anti-authority attitude exemplified by the motto, "Get Lost!" Fans, mostly tween and teen girls, can now buy a bewildering amount of Emily-branded clothes, backpacks, pencil cases, jewelry, footwear, make-up and much, much more. There's a series of comic books and young adult novels, and a feature film is in development. Apparently, real girls with black hair and cats find nothing bizarre about wearing a T-shirt of a make-believe girl with black hair and cats, but we can all agree the world is a much stranger place thanks to Emily.

EMO Not Goth.

ENGLAND Home of BAUHAUS, THE CURE and THE SISTERS OF MERCY and thus, ground zero for POST-PUNK and GOTHIC ROCK. Lucky are those who lived in the era to enjoy wearing VIVIENNE WESTWOOD T-shirts out to the BATCAVE in the early days/nights. But from WHITBY GOTHIC WEEKEND to CYBERDOG and SLIMELIGHT and the HIGHGATE CEMETERY, there is still much to be discovered there, including the second-largest serious concentration of Goths outside of GERMANY. If you're heading over for a trip, best save up and dress up.

ETHEREAL Musical subgenre of somewhat dubious origin and definition but generally meant to encompass bands with dreamy atmospherics, most often featuring angelic, soprano female vocals and shimmery, reverb-soaked guitars, as distinct from more aggressive rock or more purely sedate AMBIENT or NEW WAVE. Applied retroactively to 1980s English POST-PUNK groups on the 4AD label such as the COCTEAU TWINS and DEAD CAN DANCE during the 1990s when new artists, including Americans BLACK TAPE FOR A BLUE GIRL and Faith & Disease embraced the idea, although by this time the term DARKWAVE was more commonly used. Somewhat out of style but remains popular with ROMANTIGOTHS. *See also: Darkwave*

ETSY Online marketplace for handmade arts and crafts and a growing community of independent Goth clothing designers, jewellers, doll makers, knitters, visual artists and all-round creative types. At time of typing, more than 45,000 Goth items were listed, from elaborate STEAMPUNK brass pendants to plastic skull bunny keychains. The go-to site for unique DIY products. (The misguided ones show on up the hilariously cruel blog Regretsy.)

EVANESCENCE American hard rock group who sold a gazillion records in 2003 based on the ubiquitous radio single "Bring Me to Life." The only reason you even know or care is because of singer Amy Lee (b. December 13, 1981), a lovely dark princess with long dyed black hair who often wears tattered, VICTORIAN-style ballgowns and tight CORSETS with big boots, which helped indoctrinate a new generation of young girls into Gothdom — where they will hopefully discover some better music.

(EVERYDAY IS) HALLOWEEN Song by American industrial band Ministry, originally released in 1984 as a 12" single on emerging Chicago indie label WAX TRAX!, later reissued on the compilation *Twelve Inch Singles*. With its bouncy SYNTHPOP rhythms and lyrics all about woe-begotten Goth life, it's up there with "BELA LUGOSI'S DEAD" on the short list of universal Goth anthems, and probably outstrips the former as the single most played song in Goth clubs worldwide, not only at Halloween but, yes, everyday.

EVIL WILLOW Alter-ego of the *BUFFY THE VAMPIRE SLAYER* character Willow Rosenberg, as seen in the season 6 episodes "Villains," "Two to Go" and "Grave." Willow turns to the dark side of magic, overwhelmed with vengeful rage over the death of her girlfriend. In contrast to her usual bookish self, Evil Willow (also known as "Dark Willow") changes appearance — red hair turns black, eyes darken, creepy veins appear on her face — and transforms into a very, very bad witch indeed. The Evil Willow character remains much beloved for its power and its, well, evilness. There's even a trilogy of "Wicked Willow" tie-in novels. Combined with the "Vamp Willow" doppelgänger seen in season 3, it has made the character, and actress Alyson Hannigan, an object of affection for Goths of all persuasions. (Not to mention an excellent HALLOWEEN costume.)

EXPRESSIONISM Cultural movement from the early 1890s originating in GERMANY that set the angst-filled, melodramatic tone for the kind of poetry, art, philosophy and film Goths love to name-drop, from Nietzsche to NOSFERATU.

EYELINER Essential cosmetic item for both boys and girls — in black of course. From the daintiest cat's eye to full-blown Cleopatra/SIOUXSIE looks, in KOHL pencil or liquid paint, the cheapest and easiest way to express one's commitment to Gothness. Despite the plethora of YouTube tutorials encouraging otherwise, you might want to reconsider painting spiders and elaborate swirls on your cheeks with it after the age of twenty. Also, beware CROW MAKE-UP. *See also: Guyliner*

EYE OF HORUS Ancient Egyptian symbol of protection, as worn by the goddess Wadjet as a personification of the sky god Horus. Essentially a falcon eye crying: how Goth! No wonder it's a popular EYELINER design, even before THE SISTERS OF MERCY used it at cover art for their *Vision Thing* album. Note: traditionally the right eye represents the sun, the left eye the moon. So if you're wearing it for GOTH POINTS, choose wisely.

FANGS

FACTORY RECORDS British independent record label that gave the world JOY DIVISION. Founded in Manchester in 1978 by infamous TV presenter and impressario Tony Wilson (and someone nobody remembers named Alan Erasmus), and named for a nightclub of the same name, its first full-length record release was Joy Division's groundbreaking 1979 debut, *Unknown Pleasures*. Factory's other high profile artists include New Order, Happy Mondays and Orchestral Manoeuvres in the Dark, but apart from Joy Division they are remembered most for their unconventional art direction (album art without band member photos or even artist names, for example) and catalogue numbering system, referred to as the FAC numbers, given not only to recordings but also to everything from posters to the house cat. The final FAC number is FAC 501, on Tony Wilson's coffin.

FAIRIEGOTH A feminine, flighty, flowing dress and long hair kind of Goth, one who identifies with pixies and other mystical creatures and literally wears the fake wings to prove it. Also fond of glitter and striped tights but distinguished from the similarly dressed ROMANTIGOTHS by their ability to name the four natural elements in record time. Interested in drawing (mostly fairies) as much as listening to music. Unlike fantasy fairies, Fairiegoth girls wear pants. (Not sure I've ever met a male Fairiegoth.)

FAIRYGOTHMOTHER 1. British clothing company specializing in custom CORSETS, ballgowns and lingerie, with an increasing bent towards fanciful burlesques and high-end wedding apparel. Launched by the un-Gothily named Samantha Merry as an online shop in 1999, today also maintains boutiques in London under the name Lulu and Lush. 2. Someone who acts as a style advisor for Goths.

FAITH AND THE MUSE American musical duo, vocalist Monica Richards (she of the fancy headpieces) and vocalist/guitarist William Faith (he of the mohawk), both of notable Goth pedigree — Richards ex–Strange Boutique and Faith formerly performing with CHRISTIAN DEATH, Shadow Project and others. Debut album, 1994's indie release *Elyria*, introduced their romantic mix of acoustic GOTHIC ROCK with folk and Celtic music. By 2003, had signed with METROPOLIS RECORDS and updated to a more electronic sound, which has continued to evolve into a signature blend of dark tribal, world, rock, AMBIENT and pop, with positive lyrical themes rooted in mythology and spiritualism. Live performances are ritualistic, mystical events involving a full band, costumes, candles, dancers and other accoutrements befitting what can only be described as the most successful (only?) hippie Goth band going.

FALLS Hair accessory also known as dread falls or synthetic falls, dramatic, obviously fake extensions attached to a person's natural hair, usually as ponytails, for added length or effect and so-called for how they "fall" from the head. Can be made from human or synthetic hair or other material of choice, with wool or plastic tubing being popular, and often matted into pseudo-dreadlock style. Appeared on the scene around the emergence of the CYBERGOTH, and became one of the most distinguishing fashion features of that style, especially when made in bright neon or UV-sensitive colours and/or topped with GOGGLES. Pre-made falls are commercially available, mostly through independent craftsfolk who sell on EBAY, ETSY and other websites, though tips for do-it-yourself falls are widely circulated, and many Goths do indeed make their own.

FANGS Long pointed teeth naturally occurring in the animal kingdom on cats and dogs and spiders and viper snakes and some BATS. A prominent feature of the modern day VAMPIRE, although let's remember BELA LUGOSI never bared any on-screen so you don't really need them to portray Count DRACULA. Still, a minority of Goths will have their incisors filed down into points or implants affixed for that true bloodsucking look.

FAT BOB 1. Nickname for ROBERT SMITH, singer of THE CURE. Goth mythology says it was first coined by SIOUXSIE SIOUX after Smith plumped up quite a bit in the '90s; the U.K. press tends to use it when they don't like the new Cure record. For fans, it's not used maliciously at all, rather, endearingly. 2. The Robert Smith—style hairdo: an oversized mass of BACKCOMBED blackness.

FETISH NIGHT Club night or social gathering catering to the BDSM crowd, sometimes shortened to Fet Night, where various kinks are indulged in a public setting. A dress code usually restricts entry to those in leather, PVC, cross-dressing or other fetish uniforms; "activities" can include fashion shows, bondage demos, public spankings, etc., plus a lot of that other kind of S/M: standing and modeling. Not to be confused with a sex or swingers' club, as in general no actual sex takes place. Rather, often held in Goth bars, where Goth attire is usually acceptable for entry, although the clientele is not necessarily Goth at all. One can usually tell the difference using the assless chaps factor.

FEVER RAY Solo project for Swedish singer Karin Elisabeth Dreijer Andersson of electropunks The Knife, who released a self-titled debut in 2009 to rave reviews and much headscratching about what genre to call this music. If you ask me, *Fever Ray* is classic Goth for the twenty-first century — the eerie, unsettling sonic atmospheres, Karin's icy vocals, the bizarre lyrical narratives. (Plus her death-themed masks and make-up and gorgeous and strange music videos.) Ten years from now people will still be talking about this one, I'm convinced. A record to take to your grave.

FIALA, VYXSIN American reality TV star (née Jennifer Fiala). Came to fame as a hairstylist and waitress who, with her ANDROGYNOUS boyfriend KYNT COTHRON, participated in the CBS competition show *The Amazing Race* in 2007, and again in 2011. A PERKY GOTH in hot pink hair and outfits (the team motto was "Pink and black attack!"), she certainly smashed stereotypes of Goths as dour and funereal TRENCHCOAT MAFIA—type misanthropes. Sadly, failed to win the race's big prize but has extended her fifteen minutes of fame as model for HOT TOPIC, LIP SERVICE and others.

FICTION RECORDS British label formed in 1978 by Chris Parry, home to THE CURE until 2003 when they signed with Geffen.

FIELDS OF THE NEPHILIM British psychedelic GOTHIC ROCK band formed in 1984 by vocalist Carl McCoy, continuing in various forms to this day. One of the heaviest of the POST-PUNK lot, like a kind of SISTERS OF MERCY meets Motörhead on acid, and distinguished by a Spaghetti Western—type fashion sense involving dusty trenchcoats and cowboy hats and a Lovecraftian lyrical bent. McCoy left the group in 1991 and named his new project The Nephilim. Assorted releases and live appearances under both names as well as solo projects have left everyone but hardcore fans hard-pressed to keep up; most assume the band is a dead relic but McCoy lurks still, popping up unexpectedly and disappearing just as quickly like a kind of Loch Ness monster. Essential track: 1988's "Moonchild."

FISHNETS Tights or stockings made from a textile with an open, diamond-shaped knit that shows a lot of leg. When they first came to North America from France in the early 1900s, they were the mark of a floozy. In the 1970s, punks and then Goths appropriated the sexy legwear as their own — after they ripped them up, pierced them back together with safety pins and turned them into shirts too. Now every girl can wear them out respectably, but only in the Goth scene will you see as many boys doing it. Available in neon colours for the CYBERGOTHS, and as arm bands for the EMO kids.

FLANGE Guitarists, if you want to make your stuff sound like "She Sells Sanctuary" or "The Forest," look into this.

FLESH FOR LULU British band formed 1982 by vocalist/guitarist Nick Marsh and drummer James Mitchell. North Americans mostly know them for the 1987 pop hit "I Go Crazy" from the soundtrack to *Some Kind of Wonderful*, but they were on the BATCAVE club scene early on and released some ghoulishly fun stuff like "Subterraneans" before going for the mainstream sound with gusto. (Despite looking smashing in leather, they never were very heavy.) In 2005, Marsh told *Guitar* magazine he once hated being called Goth. "But now I actually look for myself in all the books about

Goth and think, 'How come we're not in it?'" Well, Nick, now you are.

FLESH TUNNEL A type of body piercing jewelry, hollowed-out rings generally used to show off the wearers' stretched piercings, most commonly ear-lobes. Generally made of stainless steel but can also be of bone, wood or other materials. Lighter weight than a solid flesh plug, making it handy for more extreme stretching and also allowing for additional hoops or other ornaments to be hung for fashion. Of the variety of piercings popularized amongst Goth and punk URBAN PRIMITIVES of the 1990s, they're still fashionable, especially with girls. Surprising since unlike say, that nipple ring, it's not something you can easily reverse.

FLINDERS ST. GOTH Snarky term used in Australia for a young Goth person prone to loitering around the steps outside the Flinders Street train station in Melbourne. Recently, more of an EMO or scene pastime, meaning not very Goth at all.

FLOOD British music producer (né Mark Ellis, b. August 16, 1960). The George Martin of the POST-PUNK and SYNTHPOP set. If a ten-year-old Goth/INDUSTRIAL record still sounds good on the dance floor, Flood was probably at the controls: Depeche Mode's *Violator* and *Songs of Faith and Devotion*, NINE INCH NAILS' *Pretty Hate Machine* and *The Downward Spiral*, Curve's *Doppelgänger*, Nitzer Ebb's *Showtime*, not to mention the best of NICK

CAVE and the Bad Seeds and vital new work from PJ Harvey, Sigur Ros, Goldfrapp, etc. etc. Yes, he also engineered U2's masterpiece *The Joshua Tree*. But never mind that . . . he did *Violator* and *Downward Spiral*!

FLOODLAND Second full-length album by THE SISTERS OF MERCY, released 1987. The band's most commercially successful work, breaking the Top 10 in the U.K. and spawning the hit singles "This Corrosion," "Dominion" and "Lucretia My Reflection," although the industry numbers belie its true impact: according to *Alternative Press* magazine, one of the top 10 essential Goth albums. According to me, it's #1.

FLUEVOG, JOHN Canadian footwear designer who has been crafting outrageous shoes and boots since 1985. Extreme pointy toes. Impossibly high heels. CORSET lacing or shiny metallic. A honking platform shoe called the Munster. And always secretly comfortable, even the famed, much-coveted Grand National — a boot with a cloven hoof-shaped heel. And don't forget even the inconspicuous MARY JANES have soles that resist "alkali, water, acid, fatigue . . . and Satan." A mainstream, hippie company, sure, but still to die for.

FOG MACHINE Device for the emission of fake smoke/fog, typically used on film sets, in haunted houses or at nightclubs, but if you really want to Gothify your life, buy one for home use.

45 GRAVE American HORROR PUNK band formed in Los Angeles in 1979 by singer Dinah Cancer. One of the first to combine punk, surf and a love for monster movie shock, the in-your-face band paved the way for the L.A. DEATH ROCK scene. Gained some notoriety in 1984 when the song "Party Time" was used in the soundtrack to *Return of the Living Dead*.

4AD British record label founded by Ivo Watts-Russell in 1979 as a subsidiary of BEGGARS BANQUET. Released the seminal debut records from BAUHAUS, COCTEAU TWINS, DEAD CAN DANCE, CLAN OF XYMOX and many other essential POST-PUNK, DREAMPOP and ETHEREAL acts. Art director Vaughan Oliver gave the label its distinct look (under the name Envelope 23, he designed seductive covers that did not feature the artists' faces). For many years one could pick up a 4AD release by an unknown band and be sure of its awesomeness. Switched focus in the 1990s to more American rock, and Watts-Russell has since sold it, but current roster still includes several acts fans of dark and poetic romance would be wise to check out, including The National, Blonde Redhead and St. Vincent.

FRANKENSTEIN Novel by Mary SHELLEY, fully titled *Frankenstein; or, the Modern Prometheus*, published in 1818. A classic of Gothic literature of great influence on horror and science fiction writing that has been re-interpreted for film, TV, comics, games, cereal . . . well, just about everything in popular culture. More even than the

1931 Universal Pictures classic film adaptation, the 1935 sequel *The Bride of Frankenstein* is responsible for the greatest impact on modern day Gothdom: star Elsa Lanchester's iconic black hair, streaked white and standing on its end, an amazing HALLOWEEN costume.

FRASER, ELIZABETH Enigmatic Scottish singer (b. August 29, 1963), voice of COCTEAU TWINS and, alongside SIOUXSIE SIOUX and LISA GERRARD, one of the most treasured songstresses in all of Gothdom. "Discovered" by guitarist ROBIN GUTHRIE dancing in a club at the age of seventeen, she never considered herself a singer, but her unique, otherworldly style — vocalizing emotions without using identifiable language — and soprano skills have made her one of the most influential voices in alternative music in general. Her haunting cover of Tim Buckley's "Song to the Siren" as part of 4AD supergroup This Mortal Coil set the bar for ethereal emoting to die for. Since the split of the Cocteaus in 1997, her musical contributions have been selective (to put it mildly) but there's that heart-stopping performance on Massive Attack's ballad "Teardrop," which, if it were the only thing she'd ever done, would still earn her icon status. A solo album is long rumoured/overdue; one track, the carnivalesque trip-hop number "Moses," appeared in 2009.

FREAK A not very nice word for someone who looks different from you, or has physical defects. Probably why people yell it out of passing cars at Goths. But we're not insulted. We are freaks. So there.

FRENCH QUARTER That beautiful, historic part of New Orleans that Goths everywhere dream about visiting, to drink ABSINTHE and chartreuse on Bourbon Street, score a tarot reading, wander in one's finery into a seedy alley in search of "real" VAMPIRES or voodoo gris but probably ending up at the Voodoo Museum . . . all of this stoked by reading ANNE RICE and POPPY Z. BRITE, who both injected about a million GOTH POINTS into what was already a mecca.

FUCK THE MAINSTREAM Online retailer run by the folks behind VAMPIREFREAKS.COM, specializing in clothing and accessories for teenagers — as if the name wasn't a hint. In 2006, released a four-disc box set compilation of Goth/INDUSTRIAL bands.

FUNERAL Gothic and DEATH ROCK DJ parties for all ages held in and around Los Angeles from 2002 to 2008, produced by Veronika Sorrow. A sanctuary for the BABYBATS who were encouraged to "dress to depress," especially on Goth Prom Night.

FUTUREPOP Another term for EBM music, coined by Ronan Harris of VNV NATION to describe his band's more updated (read: trancey) form of '80s SYNTHPOP and applied to the newer bands.

GOTH JUICE

GAF *See: Goth as Fuck*

GAIMAN, NEIL British author (b. November 10, 1960) working in fantasy, horror, fairytales and science fiction. Best known as creator of the long-running, award-winning comic series THE SANDMAN (1989–1996) featuring a brooding King of Dreams and his sister, DEATH. His novels include *American Gods* and the young adult story *Coraline*. His short story "Snow, Glass, Apples" re-imagined "Snow White" as a VAMPIRE tale from the point of view of the wicked witch. Both a father figure and dream date to bookish Goths everywhere, although recently married to AMANDA PALMER.

GALÁS, DIAMANDA American singer, pianist and performance artist (b. August 29, 1955) working in improv, jazz, blues, rock and more. The personification of a primal scream wrapped in dominatrix attire, known for using her multi-octave voice to demonic effect. Her debut album, *The Litanies of Satan* (1982), was based on the poem by CHARLES BAUDELAIRE and introduced her by way of shrieking, shocking experiments in vocals and electronics. *Plague Mass* (1991), a requiem for those dying of AIDS recorded live in a NYC cathedral, was a blasphemous, chilling call to activism.

Most of her music scares the shit out of most people. She has provided more palatable yet still intense vocals for Francis Ford Coppola's film DRACULA (1992) and a reading of "The Black Cat" to *Closed on Account of Rabies*, the EDGAR ALLAN POE tribute CD (1997). Influenced legions of witchy vocalists but she remains inimitable, extraordinary.

GARGOYLE In architecture, a stone waterspout in the shape of a grotesque creature or chimera, often found atop such churches as Paris's Notre Dame Cathedral. In Goth abodes, a most popular garden accessory. Knowing that a purely decorative gargoyle is actually called a grotesque is worth considerable GOTH POINTS; however, using a plastic grotesque obtained from a dollar store at HALLOWEEN year-round is minus five Goth Points.

GASMASKS *See: Masks*

GAUNTLETS A type of glove, produced in a variety of styles but most commonly covering the forearm in imitation of MEDIEVAL armour or fencing gloves. Quite versatile really: fingerless armbands made from fabrics such as lace, VELVET or PVC as worn by teen MALL GOTHS may be referred to as gauntlets, as are studded or spiked wrist or leather armbands favoured by metal types. Also a popular STEAMPUNK accessory, commonly made of leather affixed with brass or other repurposed metal tchotchke.

GAWTH Alternate spelling of Goth, used snarkily in online whining about non-Goths or MALL GOTHS who think they are GOTHER THAN THOU.

GENITORTURERS American INDUSTRIAL shock rock band and performance troupe founded in Florida in 1991 and led by medical fetishist singer Gen. Rose to some infamy amongst the underground in the mid 1990s alongside MARILYN MANSON and Jim Rose Circus Sideshow and best remembered for their S/M theme live performances. Song "Lecher Bitch" included in videogame *VAMPIRE: THE MASQUERADE — Bloodlines* (2004).

GERMANY It all started with the Visigoths and the OSTROGOTHS, those rampaging tribes from East Germany who sacked Rome in the fourth century. Then, after a long break, came Weimar cabaret and expressionist silent films of the 1920s. Actually, those things probably have nothing to do with the modern Goth's fascination with Germany, and vice versa, but for some reason, the country has always been a hotspot for the scene. Not only does it host the world's largest Goth festival — WAVE-GOTIK-TREFFEN — but clubs and clothing shops and magazines and new bands abound.

GERRARD, LISA Australian singer (b. April 12, 1961) famous as the female voice of the group DEAD CAN DANCE. Her mournful contralto vocals draw from diverse musical traditions and express a mystical quality; she often sounds as though channelling spirits in several languages, including new ones she invents herself. Since the break-up of her band, she has released several solo records, including *The Mirror Pool* (1995). She is an accomplished Chinese dulcimer player and has worked on many film scores, including *Gladiator*, for which she won a Golden Globe Award. In concert, often appears dressed in a long white gown and barely speaks to the audience. Gothdom's most angelic diva.

GHASTLY MAGAZINE Music and culture magazine published by Nosferatu Productions out of L.A. in the early 1990s. Editors' nasty feud with Sean Brennan and his band LONDON AFTER MIDNIGHT not exactly the height of journalism.

GIGER, H.R. Swiss visual artist (b. February 5, 1940). Best known as creator of the titular creature for *Alien* (1979), which was based on a painting from his collection *Necronomicon* (1977) and his subsequent original designs. His dark fantasy paintings and sculpture display a perverse preoccupation with penetration of a biomechanical kind. Possibly the first CYBERGOTH.

GLOOM COOKIE *See: Doom Cookie*

GLOOMIE A sad or mopey teenager, not quite Goth. Not widely used.

GLOOM, RUBY Fictional PERKY GOTH girl, star of the animated kids TV show of the same name about "the bright side of the dark side," broadcast on Canada's YTV from 2006 to 2008. Originally created as an EMILY THE STRANGE–type brand to sell stationary and backpacks, Ruby is the "happiest girl in the world" who is surrounded by gloomy pals like Skull Boy, her cat Doom Kitty and three ravens named Edgar, Allan and POE. A sure sign that Goth has become an archtype in mainstream culture.

GOFF Mispronunciation of Goth used deliberately as a joke to demonstrate one's self-deprecating wit, particularly in the U.K.

GOGGLES CYBERGOTHS love these things. What most people see as practical, protective eyewear used for swimming or welding, they see as the perfect accessory to be worn not on the eyes but on the forehead, usually over some neon hair FALLS. You probably can't see out of them anyhow, what with the biohazard symbol or spikes covering the lenses. One of the most striking pieces of hardware to be seen on the scene, they come in every colour and fit every size. STEAMPUNKS love them too, although they tend to make their own out of brass and leather, aviator-style.

GOREY, EDWARD American writer and illustrator (1925–2000). Oh, how do we love thee? For thy *Gashlycrumb Tinies* (1963), your tale of children meeting strange deaths, one for each letter of the alphabet ("A is for Amy who fell down the stairs / B is for Basil, assaulted by bears"). For thy set design for the Broadway production of DRACULA (1977). For anagram pseudonyms such as Ogdred Weary. For thy devilish VICTORIAN English sensibilities, and all the cats and BATS and PARASOLS in your illustrations. For thy pop-up books. For paving the way for TIM BURTON. For showing the world that a sick sense of humour can be poetic and nonsense can be art. For having your ashes scattered in the sea, to be with us, always.

GOTH *See pages 1–295*

GOTHABILLY 1. Style of punk rock music combining horror movie imagery and rockabilly as practiced by bands such as THE CRAMPS, Tiger Army and Nekromantix, also referred to as PSYCHOBILLY. Originated in the late 1970s in ENGLAND, peaking in North America in the mid 1990s and still going strong in Europe. Music is generally fast-paced, raw and may feature an upright bass rather than an electric bass; lyrical themes involve monsters, damsels in distress and assorted dead things. 2. The accompanying fashion style: slick black pompadours and CREEPER shoes for men, vintage 1950s style dresses and pin-up girl hairdos for the ladies. TATTOOS, skulls and tattoos of skulls for all.

GOTH AS FUCK Extremely, exquisitely, most definitely Goth. Commonly referring to a person but sometimes a place or thing. Equivalent of "Queer as Fuck." Origin unknown but usage widespread since around the turn of the century, when it became a popular slogan for T-shirts and buttons. Generally complimentary, a sign of admiration and respect, although it may be used negatively to describe someone believed to be stuck-up or otherwise a bit too Goth for their own good. Abbreviated in writing to GAF. *Compare: Gother Than Thou*

GOTH AUCTIONS Online auction site catering specifically to the Goth community. You won't ever mistake it for EBAY: it's designed in black and purple and the "about us" is a detailed list of their servers and network protocols, with photos!

GOTH BIBLE, THE Book on Goth culture, written by NANCY KILPATRICK and published by St. Martin's Press in 2004. One of the only sociological studies of the Goth scene to actually come from the inside, drawing on extensive first-person interviews with actual Goths.

GOTH CARD Imaginary membership card that friends will threaten to revoke for embarrassingly non-Goth behaviour (e.g., possession of a Nickelback CD).

GOTH-CURIOUS A non-Goth person, usually a teenager but not always, with an interest in becoming Goth. The Goth-Curious are generally encouraged to make contact with Goths either in person or online, to ask questions and find ways to express themselves. Not to be confused with a non-Goth person who lurks in Goth bars looking to pick up or the old lady on the bus who asks you why you wear all black.

GOTHDOM The state of being Goth, encompassing all of what is good and evil about the culture.

GOTH DRESS CODE Informal code of dress implemented at certain Goth nightclubs or events in order to restrict entry to perceived true denizens of the night. Most common rule would be "all black clothing," although more likely a list of unacceptable items (e.g., no white T-shirts or sneakers) imposed arbitrarily by the door staff as opposed to a strict definition of appropriate Goth attire. While it seems hypocritical and silly for those who fight not to be judged on their appearance to exclude others based solely on their appearance, such policies do ensure guys in EYELINER and girls in LATEX bras are safe from drunk jocks out to gawk at the FREAKS and pick up "kinky VAMPIRE chicks." This is a good thing.

GOTHER THAN THOU A put-down referring to a self-righteous Goth who considers him/herself superior to others by way of greater time spent in the scene, knowledge of music or commitment to Gothly appearance. Equivalent of "holier than thou." 2. Card game parody developed by Savant Garde Entertainment in

2000 in which the normally imaginary GOTH POINTS actually are counted.

GOTH GRANT American federal grant awarded to a youth outreach organization in Blue Springs, Missouri, in 2002 to study Goth culture in order to "combat" its ill effects in the wake of the COLUMBINE massacre. The $273,000 was provided to help identify "Goth culture leaders" that were "preying" on kids allegedly involved in "self-mutilation and animal sacrifices." As taxpayer watchdog groups were quick to point out, there were no such kids in this area and most of the money was spent on administration and shopping at HOT TOPIC. The community had little interest in attending Goths-are-people-too seminars; funding cancelled in 2004.

GOTHIC 1. A 1986 biographical film about LORD BYRON, staring Gabriel Byrne and directed by Ken Russell, recounting the story of Byron and the SHELLEYS' in-famous weekend at Villa Diodati in Switzerland, which resulted in the writing of Mary Shelley's *FRANKENSTEIN*. Russell's gorgeously lurid, enthral-lingly hallucinogenic portrayal of the events may be far from historically accurate but it took the breath away of the ROMANTIGOTHS and remains essential view-ing. 2. The easiest way to describe something Goth, for example, everything in this book. 3. A great num-ber of things from fonts to moths that have nothing to do with Gothdom. Please see your copy of the *Oxford English Dictionary* for details.

GOTHIC BEAUTY American magazine with an emphasis on fashion and beauty, featuring photo shoots and profiles of alternative models and designers, as well as product reviews and music interviews. Founded in 2000 by Steven Holiday and based in Portland, Oregon, it has become the pre-eminent Gothic publication in North America and now enjoys wide distribution through mainstream bookstore chains such as Barnes & Noble. While it's no *Vogue* in the high-quality journalism and art photography departments, it's a tireless supporter of independent Goth businesses and, with its eye-candy cover shots, the gateway into Gothdom for many a GOTH-CURIOUS teen. Since the deminse of *PROPAGANDA* magazine, the most influential print publication out there.

GOTHIC BELLY DANCE Style of dance fusing traditional Middle Eastern belly dancing with contemporary tribal belly dancing, cabaret dancing and gothic aesthetics and movement that gives a whole new meaning to "snake arms." Goth Girls have always loved Cleopatra (or at least her EYELINER) and overly theatrical dancing, but GBD is a relatively recent phenomenon, presented often as a special attraction in fashion shows or other nightclub events. While it has attracted the wrath of some belly dancing purists, a growing network of resources, including dedicated classes and instructional DVDs, are available for those who prefer their hip skirt made out of FISHNETS. May also be referred to as Raks Gothique.

GOTHIC CHARM SCHOOL Website run by self-professed Lady of the Manners, Jillian Venters, offering etiquette advice for the dark set, who she refers to lovingly as "Snarklings." Of particular interest to BABYBATS, a place where dilemmas like "Help! My parents won't let me dye my hair black!" are taken seriously and responded to with earnest concern and common sense. An accompanying book, *An Essential Guide for Goths and Those Who Love Them*, was published in 2009.

GOTHIC CRUISE 1. Theme cruises marketed to Goths. Essentially a floating weekend festival, activities include live bands, masquerade ball, fashion shows and other non-cruise-like events. SPF 1000 not included. 2. American documentary film (2008) following selected Goths on one such cruise, directed by Jeanie Finlay.

GOTHIC FICTION A genre of English literature thought to have originated with the 1764 novel *The Castle of Otranto* by Horace Walpole. Its blend of psychological terror, romance and the supernatural in a sublimely atmospheric style of storytelling is most associated with long-dead writers from the VICTORIAN era (POE, STOKER) but remains popular with contemporary authors of modern horror and thrillers, from Shirley Jackson to ANNE RICE. Typical gothic fiction tropes include haunted houses, madness and grief-stricken women in frilly nightshirts. Not to be confused with adolescent journal scrawlings about VAMPIRES who sparkle.

GOTHIC LOLITA Style of dress combining VICTORIAN gothic and Japanese Lolita streetwear, originating in Japan where Lolita is a widespread and multi-faceted subculture. In Japan it is known as "gosu rori," the most widespread of the Lolita styles; in North America and Europe, "GothLoli" or "LoliGoth" remains a fringe/fetish subset of the Goth scene but is increasingly popular with youth raised on anime. Typical outfit for girls may be a black-and-white lace dress with petticoat, frilly knee socks and PARASOL — a romantic costume in the style of a living porcelain doll; for boys, elegant aristocrat coats rule. Not actually connected with the Western Goth movement: it has a completely different musical scene and lifestyle activities include fancy tea parties or shopping, not nightclubbing. *See also: Mana*

GOTHIC & LOLITA BIBLE Japanese magazine devoted to Gothic and Lolita fashion launched in Tokyo in 1999. The world authority on the scene's latest styles, featuring photo spreads from streets of Tokyo, tutorials and sewing patterns. English language version was launched in 2008.

GOTHIC MARTHA STEWART Website spoof of domestic diva Martha Stewart, run by "Martha Gothic," filled with tips on creating arts and crafts projects for the Goth abode. Covers the standard "good things" — drying roses, stamping candles, VELVET curtains and the like.

GOTHIC MATCH Online dating service targeting Goths looking for black-hearted love. The company's ubiquitous banner ads on pretty much every Goth website in the world ensure a steady supply of sinister-minded singles. If you've always dreamed of finding your "Lucretia666" or "DarkVamp," this is the place.

GOTHIC METAL Subgenre of heavy metal music as typified by bands such as TYPE O NEGATIVE, Paradise Lost and LACUNA COIL. Generally featuring slower tempos, more melancholic/melodramatic lyrics and a greater presence of female vocalists than typical heavy metal. Sub-sub-subgenres include symphonic gothic metal, gothic black metal and so on. Considered part of the metal scene, not necessarily the Goth scene. Gothic metal bands may dress like Goths and read the same books as Goths, but Goths generally do not listen to Gothic metal music. Neither of them listens to EVANESCENCE.

GOTHIC ROCK The most popular and influential style of Goth music, and, let's face it, the reason we're all even here. BAUHAUS birthed it with "BELA LUGOSI'S DEAD" in 1979 but THE SISTERS OF MERCY adopted it, raised it, released it (mercifully) into the universe. An offshoot of U.K. POST-PUNK, it stripped that genre of its avant garde art school ambitions down to the core themes of sex and death and then, borrowing some of the macabre dressings of the BATCAVERS, presented its guitar-driven dirges with the most melodramatic of flourish. It landed in California, where CHRISTIAN DEATH took it even more seriously, and a whole new generation of American DEATH ROCKERS ran with the torch. (They haven't put it down since.) When THE CURE and Bauhaus and The Sisters say they're not Goth, they mean they are not just Gothic rock, but if it wasn't for their efforts, we wouldn't have it. While many gothy-looking kids enjoy MARILYN MANSON and Rammstein and CRADLE OF FILTH, and INDUSTRIAL is also an important part of the legacy of the subculture, essentially Goths can be defined as those who listen to Gothic rock.

GOTHIC SLUTS Website featuring erotic and/or pornographic photography of authentic gothic and punk models, launched in 1999. *See also: Blue Blood*

GOTHIC TWO-STEP The original Goth dance move: take two small steps forward, then two steps back, eyes cast downwards. Hands may rest behind the back or swirl around the head as if batting away cobwebs. Rumour has it, originated at a club in LEEDS called THE PHONO where the dance floor was so small you could only take two steps in any given direction.

GOTH JUICE I. The most powerful hairspray known to man, made "from the tears of ROBERT SMITH." So joked the British comedy TV show *The Mighty Boosh*. 2. Actual hair gel produced by Lush Cosmetics that smells like a forest. In regulation purple, natch.

GOTH KIDS Fictional characters in the *South Park* animated TV series. The four Goth Kids are Goth Leader, Red Goth, Henrietta Goth and Kindergoth, all of whom have a stereotypical Goth appearance and the cliché habits of smoking, writing poetry in graveyards, raging against "conformists" and dancing while looking at their shoes. First introduced in the 2003 episode "Raisins," in which main character Stan Marsh temporarily becomes a Goth, nicknamed Raven. They are steadfastly Goth and offended to be mistaken with EMOS or VAMPIRES.

GOTHLING A Goth child or, more likely, a child of a Goth. Not widely used.

GOTH LOLI *See: Gothic Lolita*

GOTHMINISTER Norwegian INDUSTRIAL metal project of Bjørn Alexander Brem (Lawyer by day! Prince of darkness by night!), founded in 1999. With a name like that, and a debut titled *Gothic Electronic Anthems* (2003), the missive was pretty clear. And even though the music is heavy guitar based and verging on straight metal, the dramatic make-up and skull microphone, à la Screamin' Jay Hawkins, push live performance over to the Goth side.

GOTH.NET Website resource for the Goth community. Registered in 1997 by "Raven" in Texas, it initially provided free email addresses and webspace, published gothic writing and art from its members and collected links to Goth communities worldwide. Today, mostly visited for its popular forums where more than 7,000 Goths share tips on where to buy the best black lipstick, how to deal with conservative parents or employers and, of course, What is Goth? *Compare: Net.goth*

GOTH OR NOT Humour website to which users upload a photo of themselves for others to rate their level of "Gothness." A spoof of the site Hot or Not created by Brit Jonathan Belial Jenkyn.

GOTH POINTS Imaginary game in which points are awarded for Goth-like behaviour, or subtracted for non-Goth behaviour. (Wearing flip-flops: −2 pts) Since nobody actually keeps score and there are no prizes for winning, more of a sarcastic in-joke.

GOTHS IN HOT WEATHER Photo blog run by Brit Tom Lenham featuring pictures and videos of Goths frolicking under the sun, by the seaside, and in other non-Gothy locales; photos rated for Gothiness and Sweatiness.

GOTH TALK Recurring sketch (1997–1999) on TV show *Saturday Night Live* featuring two Florida Goth teens hosting a cable access talk show that "explores the moody depths of the Goth lifestyle." Featuring celebrity guests such as Rob Lowe and Steve Buscemi acting as Goth caricatures and BAUHAUS's "BELA LUGOSI'S

DEAD" as theme music. Although the sketch openly mocked suburban teen Goth stereotypes, it was generally accepted by real-life Goths as freaking hilarious. *See also: Abyss, Azrael*

GRAND GUIGNOL Dramatization of sensationalist horror. Named for Paris's infamous Théâtre du Grand-Guignol (1897–1962), which produced shocking plays featuring gory special effects and psychological terrors. A direct influence on ANNE RICE's Theatres des Vampires, TIM BURTON's *Sweeney Todd* and those Goth fashion show narratives nobody can follow.

GRANNY BOOTS Style of women's ankle boot that laces all the way up the front, often with a short heel and rounded toe. Mostly in fashion in the '80s but still popular with ROMANTIGOTHS and STEAMPUNKS.

GRAVER Literally goth + raver. A person with Goth sensibilities who listens to dark electronic dance music and attends rave or rave-like club events dressed in much more colourful clothing than a traditional Goth, typically including neon or glow-in-the-dark hair, make-up or accessories. An American term, more commonly referred to worldwide as CYBERGOTH. A fairly common sight in the early 2000s, now on the wane.

GRAVE RUBBINGS An imprint of a headstone made by rubbing pencil or charcoal over a thin piece of paper affixed to the stone. Used legitimately by genealogists and practiced covertly by Goths when lurking in cemeteries. Pretty standard (and cheap) apartment décor.

GREEN FAIRY *See: Absinthe*

GREGORIAN CHANTS Liturgical choir music that enjoyed a resurgence in popularity in the 1990s after the chart success of Enigma's chant-sampling S/M-themed single "Sadeness." Suddenly, the Benedictine Monks were on the playlist for every ROMANTIGOTH tea party. *The Omen* theme, "Ave Satani," also remains a favourite.

GRIMOIRE Book of magic spells used by pagans in the longstanding tradition of their Middle Age ancestors. A Gothed-up name for a private journal. *See also: Book of Shadows*

GRUFTI A German TRAD GOTH. Literally an old man. Also, a "gruft." Derogatory.

GUN CLUB, THE American punk band founded in Los Angeles in 1980 by Jeffrey Lee Pierce. Steeped in blues, the band served a dirty and devilish sonic cocktail that foreshadowed such more famous POST-PUNK outfits as THE CRAMPS and NICK CAVE's Bad Seeds — both of which later enlisted Gun Club guitarist Kid Congo Powers. Still, few Goths would know of them were it not for their bassist PATRICIA MORRISON, who went on to join THE SISTERS OF MERCY and THE DAMNED.

GUTHRIE, ROBIN Scottish guitarist (b. January 4, 1962), co-founder of the COCTEAU TWINS. Known for his shimmering layers of effects bliss, the kind of swirling, SHOEGAZER sonic magic that gave legions of shy guitarists someone to look up to. After band split, founded indie label Bella Union Records with Twins' bassist Simon Raymonde. Extensive collaborations post-Cocteaus, including producing and co-writing score for Gregg Araki's film *Mysterious Skin* with Harold Budd and several solo instrumental releases.

GUYLINER EYELINER as worn by males. Goth Boys are experts at this.

HALLOWEEN

HAGEN, NINA German singer (née Catharina Hagen, b. March 11, 1955). Original punk rock queen, leader of the Nina Hagen Band who went on to a solo career in America highlighted by the early '80s club singles "New York New York" (a disco/reggae/rap/opera fusion!) and "Smack Jack" (cabaret/funk/speed/metal?) An outrageous performer and personality whose bold hairstyles careened from shocking pink BACKCOMBS or platinum mohawks to dominatrix jet black BETTIE PAGE 'dos, with provocative outfits and language to match. Her distinct operatic vocal talents and proclivity for unpredictable media stunts (demonstrating masturbation techniques on Austrian live TV in 1979, for a start) enshrined her as a female music icon early in the 1980s; in later years she voiced the character Sally in the German dub of THE NIGHTMARE BEFORE CHRISTMAS and guested on recordings by KMFDM and Apocalyptica. AMANDA PALMER fans would be wise to seek her out.

HAIRPOLICE Not what you think. Rather, a hair salon in Minneapolis founded by the late Sonia Peterson, who developed a technique for dread perms back in 1986 that has become a preferred method of achieving that perfect CYBERLOX look.

HALLOWEEN October 31. Goth Christmas. Please buy us presents, preferably in the shape of BATS.

HAMMER HORROR 1. Style of Gothic horror film produced by the British studio Hammer in the 1950s to 1970s. In particular, Goths swoon for the 1958 version of DRACULA starring Christopher Lee as the Count and 1970's lesbian-themed *The Vampire Lovers*, starring Scream Queen Ingrid Pitt. While its newer ventures (such as the 2008 VAMPIRE web serial *Beyond the Rave*) have failed to excite much interest, the classic Hammer, those atmospheric period pictures full of heaving bosoms, CANDELABRAS and CLOAKS, set the template for what Gothic cinema looked like in the pre—TIM BURTON universe. 2. A 1978 pop song by British singer KATE BUSH from her album *Lionheart*, which pays tribute to the studio.

HAND.STAPLE.FOREHEAD Phrase used online expressing (sarcastically) drama or tragedy is afoot and someone, somewhere has his/her hand raised up to the brow as in a grand, silent filmstar—like gesture, planted so firmly on the head it's as if it's stapled there. Abbreviated as HSF.

HARKER, MINA Fictional character in BRAM STOKER'S *DRACULA* — virginal, heroic fiancée of the doomed Jonathan Harker. In the novel, she suffers at the hands, and FANGS, of the Count. In Francis Ford Coppola's 1992 cinematic adaptation, she suffers from being portrayed, horribly, by Winona Ryder.

HASKINS, KEVIN British drummer (b. July 19, 1960), founding member of BAUHAUS and its spinoffs TONES ON TAIL and LOVE AND ROCKETS. The least recognizable of his bandmates, Haskins nevertheless managed to leave his mark — he does, afterall, kickstart L&R's cover version of "Ball of Confusion" with the most distinctive snare sequence in all of Gothdom.

HAUNTED MANSION Haunted house ride created by Disney in the 1960s and featured at most of its amusement parks ever since. The Rolls-Royce of haunted houses, it welcomes spooked guests into an elaborate replica of a Gothic manor tricked out with special effects ghosts and other treats laid out in various rooms, which one travels through in motorized "Doom Buggies." It has its own theme song ("Grim Grinning Ghosts"), is rumoured to have been the origin of the band name SKINNY PUPPY (apparently, the band members became enamoured with a dog character on the ride) and, since 2001, gets even further gothified each fall as the "Haunted Mansion Holiday," decorated in the theme of TIM BURTON's *NIGHTMARE BEFORE CHRISTMAS*. No wonder it's spawned its own legion of fans. The most popular attraction at BATS DAY.

HAUTE GOTH What happens when top fashion designers put girls in all-black and extreme EYELINER on the runway, spiking editorial coverage in magazines about how black is the new black. Goths drool at the photos then pin them to their bedroom walls where they wish their $10,000 Alexander McQueen dress was hanging.

HEARTAGRAM Logo for Finnish Goth metal band HIM, a combination of a heart and a pentagram. The kind of music fans who get heartagram TATTOOS (of which there are plenty) are quick to explain it was created by band leader Ville Valo to represent his ying/yang philosophy of "love metal," and not by the skateboarding jackass Bam Margera, who has since adopted it to sell shoes and such. Available on a bewildering amount of merch at a HOT TOPIC near you.

HELLRAISER Horror film released in 1987, directed by CLIVE BARKER and based on Barker's novella *The Hellbound Heart*, about a man who opens the doors to hell through a Chinese puzzle box (called the Lament Configuration) and the pleasure/pain unleashed upon Earth as a result. While the plot is ostensibly about the sometimes-cruel consequences of carnal delights, it's also about how cool self-mutilation and fetish wear looks: the heavily pierced angel/demons called CENOBITES did much to popularize S/M with the club kids. Dialogue lines such as "Jesus wept" and "I'll tear your soul apart" have become well-worn catchphrases and sampled regularly by many an INDUSTRIAL band, most notably SKINNY PUPPY. Replicas of the Lament Configuration also make fine stocking stuffers. *See also: Pinhead*

HELTER SKELTER 1. Goth/Industrial club night operating in Los Angeles from 1989 to 2002, featuring DJs and live bands, including early club shows for Nine Inch Nails. Founded by Michael Stewart and Bruce Perdew, who also ran the club Scream, its original location was the Stardust Ballroom on Sunset Strip before relocating to the Probe in Hollywood. 2. Cover of the 1968 Beatles song by Siouxsie and the Banshees on their 1978 debut album *The Scream*.

HIGHGATE CEMETERY Graveyard in North London, England, famed as home of imaginary vampires, including the (cleverly named) Highgate Vampire. In 1970, several locals reported seeing ghosts in the cemetery, with one claiming he believed a "King Vampire of the Undead" lurked there. Media hype built to the point of an actual Vampire Hunt on Friday, March 13 of that year. Highgate also appears in Bram Stoker's *Dracula* novel as the site where Lucy Westenra is buried and comes to life to stalk children. Visiting Goths may not find any evidence of the undead but can pay respects to many dead icons, including communist thinker Karl Marx, romantic poet Christina Rossetti and punk rock manager Malcolm McLaren.

HIM Finnish "love metal" band formed in 1991 by vocalist Ville Valo, originally called His Infernal Majesty. With an indie debut titled *666 Ways to Love: A Prologue*, some people had the idea the band was Satanic. The 1997 major label debut *Greatest Love Songs, Volume 666*, at

66:06 running time and 66 tracks, surely cleared that up. Like CRADLE OF FILTH, TYPE O NEGATIVE and even THE SISTERS OF MERCY before them, HIM has found commercial success mixing dark romantic lyrics with heavy guitar riffs and a hunky frontman, mostly in Europe (only 2005's "Wings of a Butterfly" ever hit in America). But with its rockist ambitions and BABYBAT fanbase, HIM caught the MARILYN MANSON curse (i.e., generally considered Not Goth Enough by most people over thirty). But I disagree: if you can find me a more Goth song title than "Buried Alive By Love" I'd like to hear it. *See also: Heartagram*

HOBBLESKIRT An extremely narrow skirt, usually below the knee or floor-length, that restricts freedom of movement in the wearer. Its popularity peaked in general North American populace in the 1910s but was resurrected for Goths and fetish markets thanks to MORTICIA ADDAMS of the *ADDAMS FAMILY*'s hobble-style gowns in the 1960s TV series. Today, those PVC and LATEX ones are not so practical for dancing, but a well-tailored hobbleskirt remains a sassy, sexy CORP GOTH choice.

HORROR PUNK Style of punk rock music attributed to THE MISFITS and practiced by their clones in which almost every song is about a monster or other creepy character from a horror film or comic and features a spirited chorus of "whoah-oh-ohs!" HORROR PUNK rockers look quite a bit like DEATH ROCKERS (i.e., one can never have too many skull T-shirts), but the music is quite a bit goofier.

HOT TOPIC If half of your high school population dresses like wannabe VAMPIRES, blame/thank this American chain of suburban mall clothing stores. Founded in 1988 as a one-stop subculture shop "all about the music," its more than 600 stores sell an extensive selection of metal, punk and Goth band T-shirts plus popular streetwear brands like LIP SERVICE and TRIPP NYC, essentially kickstarting, or at least facilitating, the MALL GOTH phenomenon. A target of much disdain from TRAD GOTHS who ripped their own FISHNET stockings into shirts, thank you very much, and guilty of pushing misguided trends (see: tutus). Hot Topic is hardly the worst thing that ever happened to Goth fashion. In fact, giving broke teens in far-flung places a chance to buy cheap PVC CORSETS and skull BUCKLE BOOTS (not to mention opening a chain of plus-sized stores, called Torrid) could be considered a community service.

HUNGER, THE 1983 VAMPIRE film directed by Tony Scott and based on a 1981 novel by Whitley Strieber. The most Goth of all contemporary vampire movies (sorry, ANNE RICE) starring DAVID BOWIE and Catherine Deneuve as a vamp couple and Susan Sarandon as the sexy doctor. Hardly Oscar material and no box office smash, but we love it so for its opening sequence featuring BAUHAUS performing "BELA LUGOSI'S DEAD" in a cage, for the special ANKH knife pendant used to slice into the necks of their prey and for having beautiful NOSFERATU who do not glitter.

HUSSEY, WAYNE British singer and guitarist (b. May 26, 1958), co-founder and lead vocalist of GOTHIC ROCK superstars THE MISSION, formed after acrimonious split from THE SISTERS OF MERCY. (Which he joined after leaving Dead or Alive.) Distinguished by his dark sunglasses and bolero hat, and his ability to take generic lyrics about darkness and dancing to the top of the charts. In 2008, released the solo album *Bare*, a mix of Mission tracks and cover tunes. Now lives in Brazil.

HYPERIUM RECORDS German independent record label operating in the 1990s, specialized in ETHEREAL and DARKWAVE and beloved for its *Heavenly Voices* compilations featuring female-fronted bands such as Chandeen, Love Is Colder Than Death, FAITH AND THE MUSE and soon-to-be headbangers LACUNA COIL.

INDUSTRIAL GOTH

IDM Short-form for intelligent dance music, a type of post-rave electronic music considered more for home listening than for dancing. The somewhat ridiculously elitist genre designation (every other kind of dance music is stupid?) originated in 1993 with a Usenet list set up to discuss recordings emerging on such British labels as Warp and Reflex, now applied to a wide variety of electronic music from AMBIENT to techno, only some of which could be considered Goth (e.g., post–SKINNY PUPPY projects like Download) Still, Goths could do worse than to listen to more IDM and less EBM, IMHO.

I'M SO GOTH Every Goth website has, at some point, run its sarcastic "I'm So Goth I . . ." list to show off how we are perfectly capable of making fun of ourselves. (e.g.: "I'm so Goth I wear sunglasses to open the refrigerator," "I'm so Goth I make Happy Meals cry," etc.) But somehow, the community seems to have settled on one joke most of all: "I'm so Goth I shit BATS." Yes, there's a T-shirt.

INDUSTRIAL Goth's meaner sibling, a style of dark, heavy music with some similar themes that's just as slippery to define, with a bewildering number of ever-evolving subgenres and sub-subgenres from avant garde to metal. Let's just say it's generally electronic, generally noisy and at its best when experimenting with unconventional construct and provocative content, although most popular when you can stomp your army boots to its beats. The term originates with British sonic terrorists Throbbing Gristle in the 1970s, is most exemplified by German scrap metal scavengers turned ballet composers Einstürzende Neubauten and can be applied to dozens of 1980s groups using synths and drum machines and shouting — although is most associated in the mainstream mind with the mid '90s industrial rock sound of NINE INCH NAILS and Ministry. While there are distinct differences between camps, the term Goth/Industrial is often used to represent where they meet, usually in nightclubs and clothing shops appealing to both.

INDUSTRIAL FISHNETS Style of FISHNET stockings with larger holes, also called fencenets.

INDUSTRIAL GOTH *See: Rivethead*

INDUSTRIALNATION American music zine, founded in 1991 by Paul Valerio as a black-and-white Xeroxed affair but well established by 1995 as a full-size, glossy-covered mag based in Chicago. Dedicated to the INDUSTRIAL, experimental, noise and, to a lesser extent, Goth music scenes at the time they were really breaking through; it was the leading source of information on new releases, with hundreds of CD reviews, band interviews and scene reports from far-flung communities (including a Toronto column written by yours truly). Despite its unpredictable publishing schedule and limited distribution, played a part in the rise of bands like Ministry and KMFDM as well as many indie upstarts it featured on compilation CDs. Lost steam around the time of the internet explosion; a 2003 relaunch failed to generate much interest.

INTERPOL American POST-PUNK band formed in 1997 in New York City. Why this band has not been more widely embraced by Goths everywhere is a supreme mystery to me. The 2002 debut album *Turn on the Bright Lights* was exquisitely Gothic: tense, intense, bass-driven death disco about urban malaise played by beautiful, morose art school boys in sharp, dark suits. And it's not like the accusations of ripping off JOY DIVISION that accompanied Interpol's arrival on the scene should have been a strike against them with this crowd. And yet, too few have recognized them and their black-and-white-and-red soundtrack to desolation and decay as the next coming not of Curtis and co. but of THE CURE. Is it because the hipster bloggers claimed the band first? Is it because the members don't dress in enough PVC? Fine then, at least those of us who love them can stand at the front of their shows and not have our views blocked by big spiky DEATHHAWKS. Your loss!

INTERVIEW WITH THE VAMPIRE Novel by ANNE RICE, originally published in 1976 and considered a Goth

Bible of sorts, popularized by the 1994 film adaptation starring Tom Cruise and Brad Pitt. The first of Rice's Vampire Chronicles series, it's set in New Orleans and narrated by undead Louis de Pointe du Lac, eigthteenth-century plantation farmer turned VAMPIRE by the sinister LESTAT de Lioncourt (a French noblemen) and also featuring their "daughter" Claudia. In it, Rice establishes an original vampire mythos that diverges from the traditional DRACULA-based narrative (garlic and stakes won't kill them, they can't transform into BATS) and presents instead the NOSFERATU as romantic, emotional, suffering creatures of great beauty and fluid sexuality with a fondness for art and fashion. So, basically, Goths. The book/film kickstarted a new era of sensitive vampire stories and further solidified New Orleans as a top choice for Goth Places to See Before You Die.

IPSO FACTO 1. Retailer of Goth/Industrial clothing and band merchandise based in California; founded by Goth singer Terri Kennedy in 1990. 2. Short-lived British all-girl band (2007–2009) with subtle Goth tendencies; keyboardist Cherish Kaya has since played with Florence and the Machine.

JOY DIVISION

J., DAVID British musician (né David J. Haskins, b. April 24, 1957) founding member of BAUHAUS and LOVE AND ROCKETS, the boy with the glasses, hanging in the background, holding it down on bass. (Stepping up to the mic on occasion, such as on L&R's "No New Tale to Tell.") Has also released music with The Jazz Butcher and several solo albums, plus worked in visual art, as a DJ, and composer of scores for film and theatre. He may not be nearly as gloomy in his solo work, but he still winks at his past, such as on the song "Goth Girls in Southern California" from his 2003 EP *Mess Up*, featuring too-true charming lyrics like: "The beach is a bitch and no fun / Goth girls don't like that California sun." Recent work includes the single "Bloodsucker Blues," with DARK CABARET singer Jill Tracy.

JEANNIE NITRO American clothing company, founded by designer Liz Tucker in 1993, specializing in TRAD GOTH and ROMANTIGOTH gowns of flowing VELVET and lace, including bridal and baby. Celeb clients include TIM BURTON and NINA HAGEN. No retail outlet, but the webstore is called The Bone Church.

JOHNNY THE HOMICIDAL MANIAC Comic strip created by Goth Boy Jhonen Vasquez, appearing first in CARPE NOCTEM magazine then published by Slave Labor Graphics from 1995 to 1997. Goth in its black-and-whiteness, its black humour horror, and its ÜBER characters, including Anne Gwish, a MORTICIA-type stick figure girl who exists mostly as both a parody and a critic of the lifestyle. The fact that *JtHM* was once sold at mall chain HOT TOPIC is a reminder of the quaint times before COLUMBINE when it was still okay to make jokes about gothy serial killers.

JOY DIVISION British POST-PUNK band, formed 1976, originally under the name Warsaw, by Bernard Sumner (guitars) and Peter Hook (bass), soon including IAN CURTIS (vocals) and Stephen Morris (drums). Some claim the first use of the G-word in a musical context was when producer Martin Hannett described their sound as "dancing music with Gothic overtones" in 1979. Some think they are the most Gothic of all because Curtis actually killed himself (May 18, 1980), as if depression and suicide are inherently Goth. No, Joy Division are heroes eternal for their small but seminal output. Two albums only, *Unknown Pleasures* and the posthumous *Closer*, that laid the groundwork for decades of sparse, eerie, baritone- and bass-heavy death disco about isolation, loss of control and love tearing us apart.

KINDERGOTH

KAMBRIEL American clothing designer of VICTORIAN-inspired elegant attire, since 1994. *GOTHIC BEAUTY* named her Designer of the Year in 2005 and her work was selected for the 2008 Gothic: Dark Glamour exhibit at New York's Fashion Institute of Technology Museum. Think bustles and mourning veils, with original updates as worn by FAITH AND THE MUSE, AMANDA PALMER, NEIL GAIMAN and others. Even *Elle* magazine has taken notice. Well done.

KAND, VALOR American singer and musician, best known as the leader of L.A. DEATH ROCK icons CHRISTIAN DEATH. What's that, you say? You thought that was ROZZ WILLIAMS? Well, that is true too. Valor, the band's original guitarist, took over the mic when Rozz left in 1985, sparking a long-standing debate about which version of the band is worth your while. (If you've ever wanted to see Goths arm-wrestle, open this question.) Many do enjoy Valor's equally provocative musings on religion, the apocalypse and sex on albums like *Pornographic Messiah*. Others find him pompous and lacking in poetry. Regardless, it is Valor who keeps Christian Death alive today.

KICKING THE SMURF Sarcastic name for the dance move in which one kicks a leg out in front or to the side, low to the ground and with great fury. (The Smurf is imaginary, obviously.)

KIERNAN, CAITLIN R. Irish-American author (b. May 26, 1964) of dark fantasy, horror and science fiction who is of great interest to Goths because she comes from inside the community herself. She even had a short-lived band, Death's Little Sister. And thus, her misfit characters (Spyder Baxter in 1998's *Silk* for just one) ring true for a change. Might be more widely known in the mainstream if her writing wasn't so raw, so filled with the kind of sex and drugs that scare away people, but in a field where it's easy to fill your stories with blood and guts, Kiernan would rather be gutsy. Also known to comic book fans for writing the *Sandman* spin-off *The Dreaming*, from 1996 to 2001.

KILLING JOKE British POST-PUNK turned Goth/ INDUSTRIAL band formed in 1978 by vocalist/keyboardist Jaz Coleman, drummer Paul Ferguson, guitarist Geordie Walker and bassist Youth. Despite the name, not all that funny. Rather, quite serious. About politics, about the occult (Jaz once moved to Iceland to escape the Apocalypse he believed imminent) and shocking the public into action, even if that meant using fascist iconography to do it. But on top of all this, an irresistible groove that has made them staples of dark dance floors through the 1980s ("Love Like Blood," "Requiem") and the 1990s

("Pandemonium," "Millennium"). Too busy with more esoteric solo projects to bother with rock 'n' roll much in the 2000s, until meeting at the funeral of one-time bassist Paul Raven in 2007 inspired a reunion of the original members. The 2010 recording *Absolute Dissent* shows they haven't lightened up much. Good for them.

KILPATRICK, NANCY American writer and editor of dark fantasy, horror, fantasy and mystery (b. May 6, 1899) now based in Montreal and known as Canada's Queen of VAMPIRE Fiction for her many, many short stories, novels and general expertise on the NOS-FERATU, most recently exhibited in the anthology *Evolve: Vampire Stories of the New Undead*. (Under the pen names Amarantha Knight and Desirée Knight, also authored horror-themed erotica.) A genuine ELDER GOTH, lover of CEMETERIES and black cats, she is also an expert on CHILDREN OF THE NIGHT, having penned *GOTH BIBLE: A Compendium for the Darkly Inclined*.

KINDERGOTH 1. An underage, usually preteen, Goth POSEUR. Derogatory. *Compare: Babybat* 2. Comic strip about a gang of sarcastic TATTOOED Goth kindergarten kids who defend the Earth from alien invasion, created around 2001 by Lee Kohse and Jeff Zugale. 3. Plush toy line by BLEEDING EDGE, issued only for three seasons around 2003 before changing the name of the line to Minor Misfits.

KING, STEPHEN American author (b. September 21, 1947). Could it be more exciting that the most well-read, bestselling storyteller of our time is a master of Gothic suspense? That he penned one of the scariest VAMPIRE tales ever with *Salem's Lot*, as well as the horror classics *Carrie*, *The Shining*, *The Stand*, etc. etc.? No, it could not! King doesn't need to wear black or write about Goths to be one of us.

KOHL Cosmetic for lining or highlighting the eyes, commonly sold in pencil form. Used since the time of Ancient Egypt and traditionally made from crushed galena, a.k.a. poisonous lead sulfide. So, plenty of GOTH POINTS even long before THEDA BARA or SIOUXSIE SIOUX started slathering it on, or EDWARD GOREY penned the lines: "the Wanton, though she knows its danger / must needs smear Kohl about her eyes / and catch the attention of a stranger / with drawn-out, hoarse, erotic sighs." *See also: Eyeliner*

KUKL Icelandic POST-PUNK band formed 1983 and best known as the first group for Björk Guðmundsdóttir. The name means "witchcraft," and their first single was a doomy, bass-driven CURE-ish number with church bells, translated as "dismembered," from a debut album (*The Eye*) inspired by the pornographic George Bataille novella. So, despite the punk rock and art school philosophical roots and jazzy, avant guard tendencies, probably more Goth than they've been given credit for.

KUTNÁ HORA City in the Czech Republic renown for its Gothness: the Gothic Stone Haus museum; St. Barbara's Church, one of the world's greatest examples of Gothic architecture; and the unbelievable Sedlec Ossuary, or "Bone Church," decorated with the bones of up to 70,000 dead souls. (No, the bone chandelier is not for sale.) The city even has an annual Gothic festival. Not as in PALE faces in FISHNETS, as in costumed kings on horses and other historical re-enactments. If UNESCO had not already declared the place a world heritage site, we would have.

LIVING DEAD DOLLS

LACUNA COIL Italian Gothic metal band formed in 1994 in Milan, formerly known as Sleep of Right and Ethereal. Distinguished by its dual male/female vocals (Andrea Ferro/Cristina Scabbia) and notable for inclusion of its biggest single, 2004's "Swamped," in the game *Vampire: The Masquerade — Bloodlines*, as well as the occasional dark romantic musings. Still, squarely in the metal world.

LANCASTER, SOPHIE English Goth Girl whose name appears here for the most sorrowful of reasons. On August 11, 2007, Lancaster, then twenty, and her boyfriend Robert Maltby, twenty-one, were brutally attacked by local youth while walking through a park in Lancashire late at night. By all accounts, the couple was targeted because of their Goth appearance; Sophie attempted to protect Robert by shielding him with her body but the attackers continued to kick and stomp until both were so injured they fell into coma. While Robert eventually recovered, Sophie remained unconscious until August 24, when family removed her life support. Public outcry was immediate and judgement was fairly swift: five boys were charged, two ultimately found guilty of murder and three of grievous bodily harm with intent; all have been imprisoned. Not surprisingly, Goths the world over responded in sympathy: benefit concerts were held, tribute videos assembled and a bench has been erected in her honour at the site of the WHITBY GOTHIC FESTIVAL. The family has set up the Sophie Lancaster Foundation and the SOPHIE campaign (Stamp Out Prejudice Hatred and Intolerance) with the aims of educating about prejudice towards alternative subcultures and having hate crimes laws extended to include "lifestyle and dress." From this horrific crime of murder came greater public awareness that it is not Goths who are inherently violent, but more often the victims of public intolerance and hatred towards those who are different, especially in smaller communities. How tragic it ever came to this. Sophie Lancaster, beautiful girl eternal, 1987–2007, R.I.P.

LARP Short for live action role playing, a kind of game in which participants act out their characters, often with elaborate costumes and immersive environments, while the rest of the world snickers. Goths joined in with gusto in the 1990s with the arrival of VAMPIRE: THE MASQUERADE, a role-playing game about VAMPIRES in a contemporary Gothic/punk universe. With the variety of LARPs dealing in vamps, horror, MEDIEVAL times fantasies, STEAMPUNK, sci-fi and beyond, there are plenty of Goths getting their geek on and having a blast with this, even though we're one of the few communities where you really don't have to traipse out into the woods with a foam sword for an excuse to wear a CLOAK and talk in Olde English.

LATEX Clothing material popular with fetish fash-
ionistas. It's near-impossible to get into, it's sweaty,
it smells — and it's a turn-on for many. Actual rub-
berists are not necessarily Goth (in fact, most are not)
but plenty of girls and boys in the scene have enjoyed
sliding into the sexy second skin that latex outfits provide. Especially since specialty designers have created
such imaginative latex clothing, from simple CORSETS
and catsuits to extreme bondage apparatus, often with
vampy or militaristic flair. And if that's too expensive:
there are always GASMASKS. *See: Demask, Skin Two*

LEE, CHRISTOPHER British actor (b. May 27, 1922),
an icon of HAMMER HORROR and the world's second
most iconic DRACULA, and the first to bear FANGS on-
screen. Also, since being knighted by the Queen in
2009, it's *Sir* Christopher Lee. Since he's had his issues being typecast as a VAMPIRE, let us also mention his
most excellent work as the Mummy, FRANKENSTEIN's
Monster, Fu Manchu and the wizard Saruman in *Lord
of the Rings*, amongst his 200-plus roles. He even has a
musical career, narrating tracks for Italian symphonic
metal band Rhapsody of Fire and releasing his own album, *Charlemagne*. But truly, the tall, dark, handsome
Lee will forever be known as the Count.

LEEDS City in north of ENGLAND (pop. 770,800), alleged Cradle of Goth Civilization. While London had
its BATCAVE and the POST-PUNK delights of BAUHAUS
and the like, it was Leeds that birthed THE SISTERS OF

MERCY. One unlikely rumour has it the origins of the term "Goth" comes from the fact that the Sisters "invaded" the British music scene from the North, much as the original barbarian Goths did to the Roman Empire in the fourth century. Most think it's enough just to be their hometown. Today, the Leeds Gothic Society maintains a presence. *See also: Phono*

LENORE *See: Dirge, Roman*

LEPZIG FESTIVAL *See: Wave-Gotik-Treffen*

LESTAT Fictional character in ANNE RICE's Vampire Chronicles; full name Lestat de Lioncourt. Star of several novels, in particular *Vampire Lestat,* which details his mortal existence as a French nobleman who is turned into a VAMPIRE in Paris, then orphaned, precipitating a spiral of sexual misadventures and "fathering" of several fledgling vamps of his own, including series co-star LOUIS — standard undead rock star behaviour. Inspiration for a Broadway musical by Elton John and Bernie Taupin. Played by Tom Cruise in the 1994 feature film. *See also: Interview with the Vampire*

LIFTS Footwear sole, commonly made from foam, which gives boots a platform height without raising the heel. A five-inch lift is GOTH AS FUCK.

LIMELIGHT New York City nightclub and concert venue operating from 1983 to 2007, part of a chain run by club kingpin Peter Gatien. For once, Goths got to play in a big budget building: a renovated Gothic church boasting spiral stairs, dark and secret passageways, a dungeon crypt, a H.R. GIGER–designed room, balconies for the voyeurs and a Goth-friendly booking policy that brought live performances by the likes of MARILYN MANSON, KMFDM and LONDON AFTER MIDNIGHT and the longstanding weekly DJ party Communion. In North America's Goth heyday of the 1990s, a mecca of sorts for those looking to see and be seen. Today, houses a boutique shopping mall. *See also: Slimelight*

LIP SERVICE American clothing company founded in Los Angeles by Drew Bernstein in 1984, now the world's most successful brand devoted to Goth/INDUSTRIAL fashion, and certainly the most rock 'n' roll. From out of the Sunset Strip punk and glam scene, Bernstein created streetwear before it was ever a term, starting with black tights silk-screened with a skull and dagger print, now a Lip Service signature. Vinyl motorcycle jackets and skin tight "Stretch F***ing Jeans" followed, as did boutiques in Hollywood. Today, thrives as a wholesaler and web retailer of limited-edition mass-produced designs catering to all FREAKS from Fetish to Cyber with a line called Black List that is GOTHER THAN THOU. Long live Lippy!

LIVING DEAD DOLLS Collectible horror-themed dolls created by Ed Long and Damien Glonek in 1998 and sold in limited-edition series by Mezco Toyz. Merchandised in COFFIN-shaped boxes and accompanied by a death certificate, they've become the most popular of all spooky toys for Goth grown-ups, who are drawn to the dolls based on untraditional themes like the Seven Deadly Sins, classic HALLOWEEN costumes or slasher movie stars.

LOLITA *See: Gothic Lolita*

LONDON AFTER MIDNIGHT American GOTHIC ROCK band formed in Los Angeles in 1990 by vocalist/ multi-instrumentalist Sean Brennan. A leader in the underground West Coast Goth revival of the early 1990s, never quite broke into mainstream but remains popular in Europe. Brennan is an opinionated rabble-rouser type, not shy to reject the G-word and fight the misconception that LAM is a "VAMPIRE" band, despite being named for a classic vampire film and once appearing on *The Montel Williams Show* about Gothic rock. Still, for legions of second generation Goths, Brendan is their ANDREW ELDRICH — for better and worse. Latest release is 2007's *Violent Acts of Beauty*.

LORD, STÉPHANE Canadian photographer specializing in portraits of Goth Girls staring off wistfully, with a particular penchant for the FAIRIEGOTHS. His work appears on the cover of MICK MERCER's book *21st Century Goth*.

LOST BOYS, THE VAMPIRE comedy-horror film, directed by Joel Schumacher and released in 1987, in which two brothers move to Santa Clara, California, and are confronted with a local gang of teenage vamps. The film's tag line was "Sleep all Day. Party all night. Never grow old. Never die. It's fun to be a vampire." It had motorcycles, taxidermy, comic book geeks and a rockin' soundtrack (theme song "Cry Little Sister" remains Goth club staple). And it made vampires cool in a way that precipitated an entire generation of stylish, bad-ass NOSFERATU young audiences could sympathize with, fantasize about. Dubious '80s fashion styling aside, icons of Goth cinema.

LOUIS Fictional character in ANNE RICE's Vampire Chronicles; full name Louis de Pointe du Lac. The titular protagonist of *INTERVIEW WITH THE VAMPIRE*, which describes his life as a French plantation farmer in New Orleans until he's turned into a VAMPIRE by LESTAT during a bout of suicidal despair. Louis, the sensitive one, the tortured one, the original ROMANTIGOTH, appears in several other Rice novels including *THE QUEEN OF THE DAMNED* and *The Tale of the Body Thief*. Played by Brad Pitt in the 1994 film.

LOVE AND ROCKETS British post-POST-PUNK group formed by ex-BAUHAUS members DANIEL ASH (vocals, guitar), DAVID J. (bass, vocals) and KEVIN HASKINS (drums) in 1985. Debut album *Seventh Dream of Teenage Heaven* featured the glorious break-up ballad of doom

"Haunted When the Minutes Drag," but L&R are the least Goth and most musical inventive — and subsequently most commercially successful — of all the Bauhaus-related projects. What with their introductory hit single being a Motown cover ("Ball of Confusion"), and their biggest hit single being a glamtastic T. Rex–style number ("So Alive"), not to mention their humourous alter egos, The Bubblemen, and their evolution into a trippy electronic act in the mid 1990s. Still, very much adored, because Goths need to smile and rock out too. Sadly, despite some one-off reunion shows, seems to be defunct.

LOVECRAFT, H.P. American writer of supernatural horror, sci-fi and fantasy fiction (1890–1937) revered as a spiritual godfather of modern horror for weird tales that redrew the cosmos as one full of nightmares. Inspired by POE yet wholly original, Lovecraft created the terrifying Cthulhu Mythos and the Necronomicon GRIMOIRE, which continue to influence to this day. Gothic literature, to be sure, but also in his embrace of the esoteric, the archaic, the dark side, a proto-Goth. He even died before he got famous. Tragic. Buried in Swan Point Cemetery, Providence, Rhode Island.

LUGOSI, BELA Hungarian actor (né Béla Ferenc Dezső Blaskó, 1882–1956), synonymous with fictional Count DRACULA. After playing BRAM STOKER's infamous VAMPIRE on Broadway, was cast as titular villain in

Universal's classic 1931 horror picture, directed by Tod Browning. Lugosi's performance — the satin-lined CLOAK, the aristocratic accent — established a new iconography for Dracula: monstrous NOSFERATU turned seductive nobleman. He did plenty more between then and his death of a heart attack at age seventy-three, but he will forever be known as the leading man vamp, as immortalized decades later in BAUHAUS's masterpiece of GOTHIC ROCK, "BELA LUGOSI'S DEAD." He was buried, wearing one of his Dracula cloaks, at Holy Cross Cemetery in Culver City, California.

LUNCH, LYDIA American singer, writer, poet, actress, photographer and all-around agent provocateur (née Lydia Koch, b. June 2, 1959) best known to punk music historians as part of New York City's No Wave scene with her band Teenage Jesus and the Jerks, or to art students and perverts as star of Richard Kern's explicit films like *Fingered*, or to women's studies types as author of the unflinching confessional *Paradoxia* or to fans of NICK CAVE and the BIRTHDAY PARTY as regular co-conspirator. But for Goths, more than for her diverse credits, she is best known for simply being Lydia: confrontational, disturbed and disturbing; a walking, sneering, screeching manifesto for DIY art and sexual liberation (including the really dark, violent sort) who made a career out of being fucked up, fucking and fucking shit up, and looking bad-ass in leather and red lips doing it. Too seedy for some but an important role model for many.

LYCIA American DARKWAVE band formed in Tempe, Arizona, in 1988 by vocalist/multi-instrumentalist Mike VanPortfleet, now a duo featuring vocalist Tara VanFlower. Architects of the American ETHEREAL sound: minimalist, melancholy, drenched in dizzying guitar effects and menaced by lurching drum machine rhythms, as epitomized on the 1993 release *A Day in the Stark Corner*, which TYPE O NEGATIVE's PETER STEELE once called "the most depressing thing" he'd ever heard. Latest release is 2010's slightly sunnier EP *Fifth Sun*. Best moment may have been spoof of *AMERICAN GOTHIC* painting for publicity photos.

MALL GOTH A Goth teenager who hangs out in malls, usually those containing a HOT TOPIC store or derivations thereof. A derogatory term for young people who make a big deal of dressing up Goth but don't know much (if anything) about the music or subculture and thus come off as POSEURS. Used more by non-Goths with a grudge than Goths themselves.

MANA Japanese rock star and fashion designer of shadowy origins. As leader of the bands Malice Mizer (1992–2001) and Moi dix Mois (2002–present) he has dressed in ANDROGYNOUS clothing and make-up, refused to give interviews, and engaged in dramatic live performances that mix classical baroque, heavy metal and Goth sounds with historical, often VICTORIAN-style costuming. In 1999, formed the clothing company Moi-même-Moitié, establishing the Elegant GOTHIC LOLITA style and further cementing his status as an icon for GOTH LOLIS in Japan and the West. If he ever decides to switch to acting, would make a great Vampire LESTAT.

MANIC PANIC Gothdom's most famous hair dye. Created by sisters Tish and Snooky Bellomo, who started importing cosmetics and hair colour into their punk clothing store in New York's East Village in 1977.

Later, concocted their own brand of semi-permanent hair dye in outrageous colours: Purple Haze, VAMPIRE Red, Green Envy, etc. These plastic jars of goo have been slathered on the heads of FREAKS ever since. (CYBERGOTHS and other clubbers love their glow-in-the-dark neon DyeHard hair gels.) Also a cosmetics line, which includes such handy items as Goth White face make-up.

MANSONITE MARILYN MANSON fan, as referred to by non-Manson fans. Derogatory. *Compare: Spooky kids*

MANSON, MARILYN American singer (né Brian Warner, b. January 5, 1969) and leader of the band of the same name he founded in 1989, who took his stage moniker from mashing up Marilyn Monroe and Charles Manson then proceeded to spend ten years pissing off parents and religious authorities all across America. You know this of course — Manson is a bona fide household-name rock star. But can he also be Goth? Of course he can. He is. He dresses it: ghastly, ANDROGYNOUS make-up; LATEX and CORSETS on stage; couture mourning CLOAKS on the red carpet. He lives it: exploring the occult, embracing perversion and decadence, collecting skulls and bones, hanging out with FREAKS. He draws weird shit. He produced a brand of ABSINTHE ("Mansinthe"). He married DITA VON TEESE, the Gothiest of pin-up girls. And he likes nothing more than to take the dark stuff most people bury and shove it right in the face of the public until they squirm. It's gotten him arrested, banned and scapegoated and still he pushed the boundaries and stood up for misfits everywhere. So why is "Is Marilyn Manson Goth?" such a hot topic? Because his band plays rock 'n' roll, not GOTHIC ROCK, and has had major mainstream success doing it. And some Goths think when the kid at the mall and the football jock who doesn't know what Goth is start wearing all black and painting themselves up like Manson it's somehow a blight on our society. Those haters might want to go watch the videos for songs like "Nobodies," "The Beautiful People" and "mOBSCENE" and think about how Manson has made some of the most gloriously Gothic pop art ever.

MARCH VIOLETS, THE British GOTHIC ROCK band, formed in LEEDS in 1981 by Tom Ashton (guitar), Loz Elliot (bass), Simon Denbigh (vocals) and Rosie Garland (vocals). Goth from the get-go: debut 7" single "Religious as Hell" was issued on THE SISTERS' label MERCIFUL RELEASE, all stern drum machine and dual ghastly vocals. Sadly, grew less and less Goth, unless you count sounding like a second-rate MISSION for a while. Key tracks: 1984's semi-hit "Snake Dance" and a rather limp cover of the Rolling Stones' "Miss Amanda Jones" for 1987's *Some Kind of Wonderful* soundtrack.

MARSDEN, SIMON British photographer (b. December 1, 1948) specializing in the supernatural. His black-and-white photography of cemeteries, churches, haunted houses and the like features in museums and galleries worldwide, and in book form on the shelf of many a Goth.

MARY JANE Shoe style for girls, distinguished by a rounded toe and one ankle strap, traditionally flat or with a low heel as worn by youth but also produced with heels or platforms. Popular with GOTHIC LOLITAS and GOTHABILLY ladies seeking the schoolgirl or retro look, respectively. Often worn with knee-high socks or striped tights.

MASKS Masquerade style masks are popular for HALLOWEEN, of course, but for the rest of the year there are surgical masks and gasmasks, available in all kinds of gothy material like PVC, for those who fetishize biohazards and other medical disasters. Like GOGGLES, introduced by the CYBERGOTHS, probably under the influence of anime/manga, and customized to sexy, sinister extremes. Laugh now, but if SARS comes back, you'll wish you had one.

MASOCHISTIC RELIGION Canadian capital-G Goth group formed and led by singer/guitarist Mitch Krol in Toronto in the late 1980s. A diabolical sonic concoction of blasphemy, poetry, S/M and nihilism over minimalist beats and grinding guitars, MR was often compared to CHRISTIAN DEATH but had a much better sense of humour about it all. Their first record was called . . . *And From This Broken Cross . . . Our Misery*;

1997 album *The Litanies of Satan* was based on the writings of CHARLES BAUDELAIRE; their performance at CONVERGENCE in Toronto saw Krol emerge from a COFFIN and set a Bible on fire. Most shocking: the guy moved to Montreal, bleached his hair blond and started a country music project.

MATRIX, THE Trilogy of science fiction films beginning with *The Matrix* in 1999, directed by brothers Andy and Larry Wachowski and starring Keanu Reeves as Neo, a computer programmer/hacker who discovers he is "The One," with superhuman powers that can end a war between humans and machines. A mainstream blockbuster success with some truly disturbing dystopian themes, this hybrid of *Blade Runner*, NEUROMANCER, anime and action certainly looked Goth: blue and grey tones, black PVC costumes and a bar (Club Hel in *The Matrix Revolutions*) based on a typical fetish club. If every Goth geek wasn't already wearing dark shades and a trenchcoat beforehand, they certainly were afterwards. *See also: Morpheus, Trinity*

MCGOWAN, ROSE American actress (b. September 5, 1973) and object of envy: not for being engaged to MARILYN MANSON for a time, but for the kind of high-end, haute Goth couture she got to wear to attend fancy events on his arm. Acclaimed on her own merits, of course: co-star of the TV series *Charmed*, in which she played a telekinetic witch; co-star of *The Doom Generation*, in which she played a red-lipped, black-haired, bad-ass punk rock girl on the run; star of *Grindhouse*, in which she played both a amputee stripper named Cherry and a car crash victim. A dream date for Goth Boys (and some Goth Girls too).

MEDIEVAL There wouldn't be Goth without the Middle Ages. Or at least, there wouldn't be Gothic. That period in Europe, from fifth to fifteenth centuries, where Gothic art and architecture was born. Oh, the flying buttresses and arched vaults! The castles and cathedrals! The stained glass and courtly love poems! The knights and the maidens! Many are the Goths drawn to this time in history — the ones who wear long VELVET dresses or carry swords to the REN FAIR, or furnish their homes with replicas of the Notre Dame GARGOYLES, while listening to GREGORIAN CHANT CDs. They might even romanticize the Black Death. Then you remind them of the feudal system, and the Inquisition, and how if born in Medieval times they'd probably be starving and burned at the stake rather than clad in finery, leisurely reading, and they have to admit it wasn't the best of times. But it sure was Gothic.

MEDIÆVAL BÆBES British classical singing group headed by Katharine Blake, ex–MIRANDA SEX GARDEN. Begun as a gang of girlfriends singing traditional songs from the Middle Ages in a cemetery in "flowing white gowns and crowns of ivy"; became a chart-topping, global sensation after release of their 1997 debut *Salva Nos*. As sassy as they were sexy, the revolving cast of six to twelve Babes brought a dark mystical sensibility to their songs and poetry, sung in Latin, Gaelic and other languages of yore. Contributed not only to the general public's hunger for new classical artists (well, at least the pretty ones) but also to Goth's renewed interest in all things MEDIEVAL. One doesn't need to like Christmas to pull out their album *Mistletoe and Wine*, one just needs to be TRAD GOTH or ROMANTIGOTH.

MELTDOWN British magazine published quarterly from 2000 to 2004, founded and edited by Natasha Scharf. Taking a high-quality glossy approach, it aimed to present dark alternative music, fashion and culture in a serious, professional light, and earned a place on major newsstands as a result, becoming the bestselling mag of its kind. Coverage varied from SIOUXSIE and Peter to J. Rock/Lolita to GOTHIC METAL. Since folding the print mag, and its spin-off TV show, Scharf has continued to bring Goth to the masses contributing to radio, TV and magazines such as *Metal Hammer*, as well as her 2011 book, *Worldwide Gothic*.

MEMENTO MORI Latin phrase meaning "remember you must die," and the art or artifacts to remind one of it. From skeletons on funereal tombs to skull jewelry and the like, the history of surrounding oneself with depictions of Death goes back in time well before modern heavy metal and Goths adopted it. Which is something you can drop when your parents tell you you're wearing one too many skulls. Or ten.

M'ERA LUNA Music festival held annually in a field outside Heldesheim, GERMANY, since 2000, featuring live performances, DJs and camping. Attracting more than 20,000 people by mixing classic DEATH ROCK and EBM bands with metal and "dark" artists. Issues "yellow cards" for bad behaviour, including crowd surfing.

MERCER, MICK British journalist, photographer and Goth music historian, author of several very important tomes: *Gothic Rock*, *Hex Files*, *21st Century Goth* and *Music to Die For*, all authoritative, comprehensive reference tools one should own, even if some information is now out of date. Probably the world's leading expert on this genre, who got his start in the trenches doing a punk fanzine, *Panache*, in 1976 and continues to cover new music for his blog while self-publishing books of rare photographs from his vaults. Full of enthusiasm but not blinded by it, you can always count on Mercer to tell it like it is: even if he believes THE CURE is not Goth, which is, of course, pure poppycock.

MERCIFUL RELEASE British independent record label formed by ANDREW ELDRITCH to release material from THE SISTERS OF MERCY, debuting with the 7" vinyl single for "The Damage Done" in 1980. Other bands on the label are generally Sisters-related: The Sisterhood, James Ray, MK Ultra, etc. Unless the band ever does put out that long overdue new recording, seems to be defunct.

MESH The holiest of Goth fabrics, used to make gloves and GAUNTLETS and also tight-fitting T-shirts for boys and the kind of girls who show off their bras, or more. DIY way to a mesh shirt is to take a pair of FISHNETS, rip the crotch out, cut off the feet and wear them upside down over your head. Not to be confused with sports uniform jersey mesh, and remember the golden rule (especially you drummers out there): mesh shirt or fingerless gloves, never both.

METROPOLIS RECORDS American record label and distributor based in Philadelphia, leading supplier of post-INDUSTRIAL electronic and Goth music. Started as a record shop called Digital Underground by Dave Heckman in 1995 importing European releases, then began licensing them for the North American market. By the time they started signing their own bands, Metropolis was so successful at understanding this market that big-name acts such as Front Line Assembly, KMFDM and Meat Beat Manifesto came calling to them. Probably directly responsible for the infiltration of third generation European EBM acts like VNV NATION and Covenant into North American clubs, as well as the dozens of copycat bands in their wake. (An "industrial 101" webpage once listed "Signing to Metropolis" as part of the top 10 things to do to become an industrial music star.) Continues to pump out new dark SYNTHPOP and other genres, notably THE BIRTHDAY MASSACRE and CombiChrist.

MIRANDA SEX GARDEN British girl band formed in 1990 as a madrigal singing group by Katharine Blake. Yes, they ultimately had boy members, and an ever-evolving sound from pure a capella to rock/classical/INDUSTRIAL hybrids involving violins and distorted guitars. But it was Blake and her female vocalists that made MSG the go-to gang for ROMANTIGOTHS seeking more edge than Enigma. Defunct. Essential tracks: "Play," "Peep Show" and "A Fairytale About Slavery." *See also: Mediæval Bæbes*

MISFITS, THE American HORROR PUNK band, formed in 1977 in New Jersey by singer/guitarist GLENN DANZIG and bassist Jerry Only. Not the first rock 'n' rollers to write songs about comic book and B-movie creatures, but their combination of hardcore and horror captured the imagination of a generation of monster kids. Remains a seminal act for fans of DEATH ROCK and GOTHABILLY, with a ubiquitous skull logo. *See also: Crimson Ghost; Devilock*

MISSION, THE British GOTHIC ROCK band (also called The Mission U.K. in North America) formed in 1986 by WAYNE HUSSEY and Craig Adams after they left THE SISTERS OF MERCY, not without acrimony. Enjoyed significant chart success with '86 debut *God's Own Medicine* and delivered steady stream of bombastic, arena-sized rock well into the 1990s. In hindsight, they were never actually all that good, and few in the next generation have bothered with them. Still, for a time, one of the biggest bands in all of Gothdom. No idea why they named 2010's album *Dum Dum Bullet* (lifted from the lyrics to Sisters' hit "Lucretia") unless Wayne and ANDREW ELDRICH have an in-joke going that eludes the rest of us. Key songs include "Wasteland," "Severina," "Tower of Strength" and covers of "Dancing Barefoot" and "Like a Hurricane."

MODERN PRIMITIVES Practitioners of BODY MODIFICATIONS such as TATTOOING, piercing and scarification, specifically urban Westerners interested in the spiritual or more traditional rite of passage elements. Popularized by the 1989 book of the same name by RE/SEARCH PUBLICATIONS, which exposed some fairly radical mods such as genital piercings, extreme CORSETRY and flesh hook suspension to a wider audience. By the time Lollapalooza brought the Jim Rose Circus Sideshow all across North America in 1992, some of these things were well on their way from the underground to the mall. Now that they are out of fashion, Goths can go back to feeling rebellious and transgressive for having their nipples pierced.

MODERN VAMPIRE A person who believes that VAMPIRES exist, and they are one of them. Communities of sanguinarians (those who drink blood) and psychic vampires (those who drain lifeforce/energy instead) pretty much play amongst themselves, either in actual churches/cults or in online groups. A complicated topic. I'd say most if not all are delusional, but since they have very little to do with Goth other than public stereotype, I can get away with avoiding further detailed discussions on the matter and instead direct you to the books *American Vampires: Fans, Victims, Practitioners* by Norine Dresser and *Vampire Nation* by Arlene Russo.

MOONBOOTS Generic term for a huge honking boot: usually with a raised, though flat, platform sole and many buckles. Not to be confused with the actual trademarked "Moon Boot" which is a shapeless ski boot type of thing. *See: Demonia, Transmuter*

MOPEY GOTH The most stereotypical Goth of all, one who wallows in melancholy, exhibits anti-social behaviour and would rather be left alone in the darkest corner of the café clutching a BAUDELAIRE or writing tortured poetry to the point where even other Goths will tell them they should cheer up. There are fewer of these than you might think.

MORBID CURIOSITY American magazine publishing first-person essays on unusual activities, edited by Loren Rhoads, from 1997 to 2006. Often macabre and grotesque (necrophilia!), developed a cult following. Most Goth? The mag held its own wake. The anthology *Morbid Curiosity Cures the Blues* was published in 2009.

MORBID OUTLOOK Goth culture webzine published by writer/DJ Mistress Laura McCutchan, begun as an old-school cut-and-paste zine out of New York City in 1992, now based in Toronto. One of the earliest to jump online, where it continues to publish original fiction and poetry alongside reviews, interviews and features about music, art, fashion and a healthy Goth lifestyle, including veganism and spirituality.

MORPHEUS 1. Alias for the character Dream in NEIL GAIMAN's comic book series *The Sandman*, named for the Greek god of dreams and drawn as a tall thin man with stars in the black holes where his eyes should be. Not as important to Goths as *Sandman*'s DEATH character (obviously) but still inspiration for many an online pseudonym. 2. Fictional character in THE MATRIX trilogy of films (played by Laurence Fishburne), a terrorist, a ship's captain, a pill pusher, a sporter of trenchcoats.

MORRISON, PATRICIA American musician (b. January 14, 1962) best known as the bassist for THE SISTERS OF MERCY during The Sisterhood/*Floodland* era and member of the proto-Goth outfit THE GUN CLUB. Her seductive, vamp-like appearance — red lips, black EYE-LINER, huge, huge BACKCOMBED hair and a penchant for slick, tight-fitting fetish wear and stiletto boots — made her a Goth Girl style icon, probably only second to SIOUXSIE, in the 1990s. Her Sisters stint was short-lived but in 1996 she joined THE DAMNED, later marrying singer DAVE VANIAN and, in 2004, had what might possibly be the world's most beautiful Goth child, Emily Vanian. Currently retired from music.

MORTICIA Fictional character created by cartoon-ist Charles Addams in the 1930s, matriarch of the ADDAMS FAMILY. She's become the archetypical Goth woman for a reason: her PALE skin and extra long black hair is bewitching; her tight-fitting, HOBBLESKIRT-ED black gown with octopus tendril tails is sexy; and her penchant for carnivorous plants (or cutting the heads off roses) displays both domesticity and wicked-ness. Most famously brought to life by Carolyn Jones for the 1960s TV series, but also by Anjelica Huston in the 1990 feature films. Alongside ELVIRA, prob-ably the #1 image in the public mind when they think "Goth" — judging by how often we all get cat-called "Hey, Morticia!" No matter how annoying the heck-ler, most of us consider this a compliment.

MOSHER I. Someone who is moshing, i.e., aggres-sively slamming his/her body into other moshers or pushing each other around in the front "pit" at a punk or metal show. In use since the early 1980s and attrib-uted to D.C. hardcore act Bad Brains. Not something Goths do, which is why the following is confusing. 2. In ENGLAND in the 2000s, became a derogatory term for young misfits — sometimes Goth, sometimes EMO, sometimes metal — who dress in black baggy pants and band T-shirts and hang about in public squares with not much to do except hate-on "chavs" (working class delinquent types who wear a different type of baggy pants). Goths are sometimes erroneously referred to as "moshers" by the lazy English media.

MUGLER, THIERRY Austrian fashion designer (b. December 21, 1948) who brings fetish to the runway: CORSET gowns, LATEX dresses (for girls and boys), even plastic and chrome, in exaggerated geometric shapes that celebrate, punish and re-imagine the body. At times gloriously combining stern Victoriana with high-tech sci-fi, Mugler is dramatic, decadent, deviant. So what if he uses bright colours? Still belongs in our (fantasy) closets.

MUNDANE A normal person, not belonging to any particular alternative subculture, as seen by a Goth or other FREAK. Assumed to live a rather boring life. Not widely used amongst adults.

MUNSTERS, THE Fictional TV family of monsters, headed by Lily Munster, a VAMPIRE with long black hair with a shocking white stripe, and Herman Munster, a lumbering, lovable *FRANKENSTEIN*-type creature, who live in a Gothic mansion at 1313 Mockingbird Lane. *The Munster*s sitcom was a spoof of stereotypical American family values, broadcast from 1964 to 1966; in syndication it developed a cult following. Lily Munster, like VAMPIRA before her, became a Goth matriarch. Herman is just a cool ghoul. *See also: Addams Family*

MURPHY, PETER British singer (b. July 11, 1957), widely considered the Godfather of Goth for fronting BAUHAUS, and rightly so. His appearance singing

"BELA LUGOSI'S DEAD" in the opening sequence of the film *THE HUNGER* — seductive, cadaverous, caged, enshrouded in fog, the baritone voice a siren song to the dark side — has probably done more to turn people on to that band, that sound, that look than anything else that came crawling out of the BATCAVE club. He is also Lord of the Goth Dance, a student of the artform who has always used the body as part of his show. His biggest hit in North America came on his 1990 solo album *Deep*, with the acoustic guitar modern rock radio hit "Cuts You Up," after which he gradually slunk back into the shadows — moving to Turkey, converting to Islam, releasing more solo albums that defied expectations. And if he can never quite escape the Goth tag at least he's having fun with it: when Trent Reznor asked him to make a special appearance at one of NINE INCH NAILS' farewell concerts in 2009, he emerged on stage from the ceiling, suspended upside down like a BAT! And oh, those cheekbones. Here's hoping his cameo in 2010's *The TWILIGHT Saga: Eclipse* movie will bring the next gen into the fold.

MUTE RECORDS British record company, founded by Daniel Miller in 1978 and most famous for signing Depeche Mode but also home to NICK CAVE, Nitzer Ebb, CABARET VOLTAIRE, DIAMANDA GALÁS, Laibach, DAF, Einstürzende Neubauten, MIRANDA SEX GARDEN, etc., etc. Truly, titans of the industry, with a dedication to synth-based music in particular (a sublabel, NovaMute, handles more experimental electronics), and the ability to take dark souls with unconventional artistic visions and make them as close to mainstream stars as this genre gets. Even better: they continue to release new innovative acts as exciting in this day as THE CURE and THE SISTERS were back in theirs — Goldfrapp, FEVER RAY, A Place to Bury Strangers and more. May they never go silent.

NINE INCH NAILS

NDH Neue Deutsche Härte, musical subgenre, translates to "new German hardness." Coined to describe Rammstein's mix of metal and electronic music and applied to several heavy German acts with strong male vocals and repetitive lyrics, most notably Oomph! Not widely used in North America.

NECK CORSET Stylized brace or collar worn around the neck for decorative or bondage purposes. Can be made from any material but most effective when includes boning and tight lacing that constricts wearer's head mobility; popular in leather. In its most extreme form, covers the bottom half of the face to restrict speech as well. Most commonly worn by females.

NECROMANCE Natural history store and cabinet of curiosities opened in Los Angeles in 1991 specializing in dead things: beetles and bones and BAT skeletons. Expanded to a second location in 2006, offering more VICTORIAN mourning wear, antique medical instruments, etc., as well as the typical SILVER jewelry and skull knic-knacks. A one-stop crypt furnishing shop.

NECROPOLIS Large cemetery or burial ground, originally specific to an ancient civilization but now applied to everything from Egyptian tombs to the Parisian

Panthéon to the Arlington National Cemetery in Washington. For Goths, a perfect place for a late night stroll, or a name for your club night, as has been done around the world from Florida to Tokyo.

NEFFS Nickname for FIELDS OF THE NEPHILIM, used affectionately, mostly by the British press.

NEMI Norwegian comic strip created by Lise Myhre in 1997, starring wisecracking Goth Girl Nemi Montoya. Nemi is PALE skinned and raven haired, listens to heavy metal and Goth music, hangs out in pubs with her blue-haired best friend and swears alot. Her father likes :wumpscut:. No wonder it's been translated for the British market, as well as newspapers all across Europe. Three graphic novel books are available in English. She could kick EMILY THE STRANGE's ass.

NEO-CLASSICAL Subgenre of DARKWAVE describing bands with classical influence, often featuring female vocals, acoustic/orchestral instruments or arrangement and flair for the MEDIEVAL. A bit of a dubious term really, seemingly created to define DEAD CAN DANCE and now applied to a bunch of underground bands to which the term new age surely would suffice, by folks who know little about actual classical music. Nothing to do with legit neoclassicism in art and music studies.

NET.GOTH Most simply, a Goth who spends time on the internet. Originally coined for users of the

ALT.GOTHIC.NET Usenet group by member SEXBAT, then expanding to describe users of all gothy Usenet groups, then ultimately all net users at large. Since that would now describe pretty much every Goth in existence (even those literally living in caves under rocks) it's pretty much out of use.

NETTWERK Canadian record company based in Vancouver, B.C., founded in 1984 and best known as the label that launched SKINNY PUPPY into the world, as well as signing or distributing other significant underground Goth/INDUSTRIAL acts of the day including Tear Garden, Rose Chronicles, Consolidated, Bel Canto, etc. Consistent art direction from Steven Gilmore made Nettwerk a North American 4AD of sorts for a while. Oh, then their new signing Sarah McLachlan sold a gazillion records and they turned their attention to finding other female singer-songwriters who would do the same. Still has Delerium and Conjure One and released Peter Murphy's 2011 solo disc *Ninth*, but otherwise off the Goth radar.

NEUROMANCER Science fiction novel by Canadian author William Gibson published in 1984. Gothic themes throughout its dystopian world, plus coined the term "cyberpunk," launching it as a literary genre. CYBERGOTHS: meet your maker.

NEWGRAVE American magazine devoted to the California DEATH ROCK scene, edited by Matt Riser and published from 2000 to 2003. Distributed free in the L.A. area and sold across America through HOT TOPIC and Tower Records. One of the few North American publications to pay attention the rising Jrock/VISUAL KEI scene.

NEW ROCK Footwear company founded in Spain in 1978, famous for its heavy metal boots. Like, literally metal-plated. The thick rubber soles and platforms, adorned with spikes, flames, skulls and other biker-worthy fixins help the RIVETHEAD boys and girls get their Mad Max on.

NEW ROMANTIC Music and fashion movement of the late 1970s in the U.K. that gave way to NEW WAVE in the '80s and, ultimately, ROMANTIGOTHS in the '90s. A colourful, flamboyant and ANDROGYNOUS response to punk, born in the clubs, not the streets — where costuming and dancing was more important than rabble rousing. Most New Romantic bands were too straight-up pop to be Goth (e.g., Duran Duran, Spandau Ballet) although ADAM ANT straddled the line. Its legacy is stronger on the fashion side: the origins of the English frilly POET SHIRT revival are found here.

NEW WAVE Musical genre originating in the U.K. in the late 1970s, initially synonymous with punk then used to describe acts either more experimental or more pop, then used in North America for all new bands from Britain, then used synonymously with

SYNTHPOP. Almost everyone with a funky hairdo and a radio hit was tagged as new wave in the '80s but when Goths speak of it they're usually talking about acts like ABC, The Human League and Yazoo, whose music continues to be spun, not totally without irony, at clubs today.

NICE BOOTS . . . As in "Nice boots. Wanna fuck?" The Goth pick-up line of choice. Started as a joke on ALT.GOTHIC, now so standard you can buy the T-shirt. (In case you're too shy to actually say it aloud.) CORP GOTHS reinvented this joke as "Nice stock options . . ."

NICE HAIR Webcomic created by Vancouver artist A. Mauchline in which NEIL GAIMAN, ROBERT SMITH and TIM BURTON are roommates! They all have nice hair, get it?

NIGHTBREED 1. British record label, founded in Nottingham by Trevor Bamford in 1990 initially to put out one compilation of new underground Goth bands, grew to a full-blown label and distributor. Its compilation series, *The Gothic Sounds of Nightbreed*, remains a nice audio snapshot of the scene of the 1990s, featuring otherwise forgotten bands like Suspiria and Midnight Configuration. In August 2010, Bamford helped launch Nightbreed Radio, an online station streaming Goth/INDUSTRIAL/alternative music. 2. 1990 horror film by CLIVE BARKER based on his novella *Cabal*.

NIGHTMARE BEFORE CHRISTMAS, THE Stop-motion animated musical film co-written by TIM BURTON and directed by Henry Selick, released 1993. The dreams of every Goth Girl and Boy come to life: HALLOWEEN Town!! Macabre musical numbers!! VAMPIRES, ghouls, ghost dogs! Basically, the *It's a Wonderful Life* of Gothdom, dusted off each Halloween, Christmas and many nights in between to relive the story of sensitive, striped-suited Pumpkin King JACK SKELLINGTON opening a portal to Christmas Town. Knowing every word of the theme song, "This Is Halloween," by Danny Elfman is a given. No amount of NBX merchandise is too much: not the pillowcases or socks or nightlights or lunchboxes or cookie jars. Who cares that it's Disney? Their money gave us the *Nightmare*-themed HAUNTED MANSION Halloween event, and a 3-D version in 2006. Dare I say, romantic interests who do not enjoy this film should be tactfully reconsidered.

NIGHTWISH Finnish symphonic GOTHIC METAL band formed by keyboardist Tuomas Holopainen in 1996. That an act mixing metal, opera, weepy power ballads, keyboard solos and fantasy lyrics about Tolkien and STEPHEN KING could be a global commercial success probably has something to do with the fact that former singer Tarja Turunen is one of the most attractive women in rock. Despite the metal guitars, a little lightweight. Still, your preteen niece could do worse.

NIN *See: Nine Inch Nails*

NINE INCH NAILS American INDUSTRIAL music project led by multi-instrumentalist/vocalist/composer Trent Reznor since 1988, commonly abbreviated as NIN. Half the people reading this book worship the guy; the other half strongly believe he's not at all Goth and would sword-fight you about it. Count me Team Reznor: as the most commercially successful industrial music artist of all time, he's done more to put that genre out into the universe than everyone else combined. He's genuinely emotionally tortured (or was, when he wrote hits like the universal ballad of despair "Hurt") and bleeds his self-deprication, his depression, his social anxieties into violent, noisy, eerie, erotic sonic experiments that you can sing and dance along to. If JOY DIVISION is Goth, so is NIN. There's also the visual presentation, from high tech stadium wizardry to the rocking of LATEX outfits at Woodstock '94. And re-introducing PETER MURPHY to a whole new generation by booking him as opening act on the NIN farewell tour. Sure, Reznor is kind of humourless when he's screaming out, "Head like a hole! Black as your soul!" but his canon is vast and will play on at every Goth disco long after he's gone. I'd find it hard to believe you're reading this book without a copy of 1994's *The Downward Spiral* in your music library. (May I also suggest the 1999 double-disc masterpiece *The Fragile*?)

NINNY A fan of NINE INCH NAILS, used derogatively by those who don't believe NIN to be Goth, and therefore their followers the ultimate POSEURS. *Compare: Mansonite*

NME *New Musical Express*, British music newspaper founded in 1952 (yes, really!), which covered the Goth movement since before it even had a name. For example, *NME* reviewed the first JOY DIVISION gig in 1979, and published an article declaring bands like SIOUXSIE AND THE BANSHEES and SEX GANG CHILDREN to be "positive punk" in 1983. Plenty of snarky yet supportive ink on the scene followed for years. But in a 2004 special issue, they also declared Goth died in 1992. Pity.

NOIR LEATHER Retailer of fetish clothing specializing in leather, in Detroit area since 1981. Long before bondage wear and punk accessories were available at every mall in the world, Noir was catering to the BDSM and Goth crowd with provocative ads featuring its distinctive skull and crossbones logo. It maintains a strong presence in the Detroit community with its regular FETISH NIGHT, Hellbound. Loss of GOTH POINTS for sponsoring the bikini car wash though.

NORMAL, THE Recording project for Brit Daniel Miller, better known as the founder of MUTE RECORDS. A one-hit wonder known for its 1978 track "Warm Leatherette," a provocative, pulsing minimalist electronic number about fetishizing car crashes based on the J.G. Ballard novel *Crash*. Covered by NIN's Trent Reznor and PETER MURPHY on their 2006 tour.

NOSE CHAIN Jewelry chain connecting a nose ring to an earring along one side of the face. Traditionally worn by women in India, adopted by some Goths and punks in the 1980s. Rarely seen today, although singer Anna-Varney Cantodea of the German band SOPOR AETERNUS AND THE ENSEMBLE OF SHADOWS has popularized it somewhat in the modern DARKWAVE scene.

NOSFERATU 1. Romanian word for "VAMPIRE," at least according to BRAM STOKER's *DRACULA*; actual etymology is in dispute. Generally used as a synonym for vampire. 2. EXPRESSIONIST German silent film from 1922, a.k.a. *Nosferatu, eine Symphonie des Grauens*, a.k.a. *Nosferatu: A Symphony of Horror*, a.k.a. *Nosferatu: A Symphony of Terror*, a.k.a. the go-to video projection for your HALLOWEEN party or club night. Directed by F.W. Murnau and starring Max Schreck as the sinister, rat-like Count Orlok — the studio's way of shooting what is essentially Stoker's story without having the rights to do so. A glorious black-and-white production that, in its final scene, created the notion that vamps are killed by sunlight. Seminal. 3. *Nosferatu the Vampyre*, 1979 remake of the 1922 film by German director Werner Herzog, starring Klaus Kinski. 4. English GOTHIC ROCK band formed 1988 by guitarist Damien DeVille. Carried the torch for unabashed SISTERS-styled sonics and spookshow concert theatrics throughout the '90s, becoming one of the most successful second generation bands to break through in the U.S., with releases on DANCING FERRET and CLEOPATRA, and ex-DAMNED drummer Rat Scabies guesting on 1998's *Lord of the Flies*. Imagine: a Goth band that actually enjoyed being Goth! Recording output has slowed and current influence is negligible but band continues to tour festivals; DeVille's autobiography, *Vampyre's Cry: The History of a Gothic Rock Band*, is forthcoming.

NO WAVE Music and art movement emanating from the New York underground in the late 1970s, a nihilistic, noisy kick at the darkness that had little to do with Goth proper but is cited by plenty of art school students as inspiration for their nonsensical film projects. *See also: Lunch, Lydia*

NURMI, MAILA *See: Vampira*

OGRE

OGRE, NIVEK Canadian singer/actor (né Kevin Ogilvie, b. December 5, 1962) generally referred to as Ogre. Best known as the vocalist for SKINNY PUPPY, although the type of vocalizing he's famous for would hardly be called "singing" by most people's parents: guttural, heavily distorted, scream-of-conscience howling that suits his stage moniker. His live performance style is a horror film made flesh: MASKS, fake blood, throwing himself into terrifying set pieces about vivisection and other gruesome delights. Distinguished guest on albums from KMFDM, Pigface, Revolting Cocks, etc.; released solo and side-projects under the names W.E.L.T., Rx and ohGr. Recently stepped into acting, notably in the *REPO! THE GENETIC OPERA* musical. A prankster, a recovered drug addict, an animal rights activist, an icon.

OONTZ! The sound of a repetitive heavy dance beat, used to describe a particularly generic style of INDUSTRIAL music often heard at clubs, much to the dismay of the GOTHIC ROCK fans. Referring to something as "oontz-oontz music" is generally derogatory.

ORKUS German music magazine, published since 1998, covering Goth, INDUSTRIAL, metal and other sounds from the dark side. Striking ÜBERGOTH cover photos and accompanying compilation CDs of new bands have helped make it one of Europe's top alternative music publications. Since 2006, available sporadically in English as well, although never quite taking hold in North America.

OSCURO/OSCURA Spanish term for a Goth Girl/Boy, used in Mexico. Literally, dark.

OSTROGOTH The Original Goths, one of two branches of third-century East Germanic tribe that first used the G-word (the other being Visigoths). Some modern Goths think knowing about the history of their battles gives you GOTH POINTS. But unless you're a real VAMPIRE and were actually on the scene way back then, it's hardly worth talking about.

OUTBURN American music magazine, published bimonthly and edited by Octavia Laird, which begun as a superb Goth/EBM/INDUSTRIAL zine in 1996 covering the likes of Swans and ALIEN SEX FIEND but quickly devolved into a more mainstream alternative/metal publication, featuring indie, EMO and whatever else the HOT TOPIC kids might be into. Can't blame them for wanting to get paid, but a loss for the Goths.

PRICE

PAGE, BETTIE American pin-up model (1923–2008) known as the "Dark Angel," famous for her bondage pictorials taken in the 1950s. In her jet black hairdo and the highest of heels, she exhibited a delight in being tied up and spanked by other girls, or playing the dominatrix role. She disappeared from the spotlight afterwards, converting to Christianity, but a revival in the late 1980s put her image front and centre at the same time that Goth and fetish cultures were emerging from the underground, and she became a style icon whose look continues to be emulated today by GOTHABILLY girls everywhere. 2. Women's hairstyle featuring short, razor straight bangs and shoulder-length waves, named for 1950s pin-up starlet and popular amongst retro-loving Gothabilly girls.

PALE The preferred shade of skin colour, whether you're Caucasian or not. Alabaster. Ivory. Extreme whiteface. Goths have always enjoyed playing with shadows, and the lightest skin matched with jet black hair and clothes has become a kind of uniform. Few take this to the point of skin bleaching — although we like reading about those old arsenic- or lead-based whiteners favoured by damsels of yore — but staying out the sun, wearing a high SPF and even carrying a PARASOL is considered wise. Cosmetics provide an extra lift: unlike the general populace, many Goths deliberately use a shade or two lighter than their natural skin tone. Clownishly applied HALLOWEEN-grade white face paint is a rite of passage for many teen Goth boys, though they mostly grow out of it. Bonus: when done properly, makes you look like the undead.

PALMER, AMANDA American singer and musician (b. April 30, 1976) best known as one half of THE DRESDEN DOLLS and affectionately called "Amanda Fucking Palmer" by her fans. A former busker, she has combined theatrical arts with music in various projects (including Evelyn Evelyn, a duo claiming to be conjoined twins) and her cabaret-punk look has been adopted by much of the current generation of ROMANTIGOTHS and STEAMPUNKS. Her confessional blog and Twitter postings have made her legions of virtual friends, thousands of whom came to her defense when her label Roadrunner Records tried to edit one of her vids, claiming she looked too fat. They're not the only ones to think she's just perfect as is: Palmer recently married author NEIL GAIMAN.

PARASOL Portable canopy to shade oneself from the Yellow Hurty Thing (the sun). Popular with ROMANTIGOTHS and GOTHIC LOLITAS, who often customize cheap paper parasols with black paint, lace trim, etc.

PEEL, JOHN British radio DJ (1939–2004) beloved as champion of new underground music on BBC from the 1960s until his death. His Peel Sessions recordings with artists such as THE CURE, JOY DIVISON, SIOUXSIE, BAUHAUS and ALIEN SEX FIEND remain telling audio documents of the birth of POST-PUNK and Goth. His remains are buried at St. Andrew's Church in Suffolk.

PÈRE LACHAISE Parisian cemetery, the city's largest and one of the most visited in the world. Acres upon acres of twisting walkways filled with the final resting places of more than 300,000 bodies, housed in tomb and crypts and columbariums of varying states of grandeur and/or decay. No wonder it's a vacation hotspot for the PALE set, who come not so much for the famous graves (although there are many: Oscar Wilde, Colette, Jim Morrison, Chopin, etc.) but to wander amongst its deathly splendour, listen to the call of ravens and take a photo of the weeping widow sculpture on Raspail's tomb, as seen on the cover of DEAD CAN DANCE's *Within the Realm of a Dying Sun* album.

PERKY GOTH A Goth who smiles. No, seriously. Some Goths like dressing up in pink, cracking jokes and otherwise smashing all the stereotypes. There is no particular style of dress or music mix that unites them, rather, it's their positive outlooks and ability to have a fun time while others are scowling about in the shadows. Prone to bouncing.

PERMISSION American magazine edited by Jayson Elliot from 1992 to 1997. Originally a black-and-white zine, it quickly became the leading North American glossy publication devoted to the scene during its heyday, although its publishing schedule was somewhat erratic. Published hundreds of album reviews plus interviews, comics and cheeky features like "Why'd you get kicked out of Denny's?" that reflected the attitude of the culture as well as its art. Relaunched in 2004 as a not-at-all-Goth general lifestyle and fashion mag in NYC.

PERRETTE, PAULEY American actress, poet and singer (b. March 27, 1969) who portrays Perky Goth criminal investigator Abby Sciuto on the network drama *NCIS*, a character that walked straight out of a Hot Topic and is probably the most famous Goth, real or imagined, of the twenty-first century. The question "Is Pauley Perrette actually a Goth in real life?" has replaced "Is Marilyn Manson Goth?" as the most pressing issue of our time, apparently. She insists she is not, but let's take a look: jet black Bettie Page hair, tattoos, writes poetry, animal rights activist, obsessed with crime scenes. Could go either way, really. But her band, Lo-Ball, isn't Goth. And she has completely avoided joining MySpace, Facebook, Twitter and the like, which might make her the only Goth Girl on Earth to do so. So I guess she'll remain the stuff of TV dreams, folks.

PHONO Nightclub in Leeds, ground zero hang-out for original goth stars The Sisters of Mercy and

THE MARCH VIOLETS and most if not all of the other pasty-faced crowd in town. Catering to misfits since it was a hippie/rocker bar in the 1970s, became home to the Goth set in early 1980 when it was known Le Phonographique, later continuing the legacy in the 1990s as Bar Phono with its Black Sheep Sunday DJ nights. The Sisters' song "Floorshow" was apparently inspired by the dancing denizens of the subterranean dive bar, which boasted central pillars for one to do the hokey-pokey around. Apparently, the GOTHIC TWO-STEP dance was born here as well. Not as well known as the BATCAVE, but for those who were there, just as legendary.

PICK THE APPLE Dance move in which the Goth reaches one hand up to the sky and seems to pluck an invisible object from the air with a melodramatic turn of the wrist. The advanced version of the move is known as "Pick the Apple, Take a Bite, Oh No! That Tastes Poisonous! Throw It on the Ground and Stamp It With Your Foot. Oh, Look! I've Located My Lost Contact Lens." *See also: Gothic Two-Step, Kicking the Smurf, Sweeping the Floor*

PIKES *See: Winkle pickers*

PINHEAD Fictional character from CLIVE BARKER'S HELLRAISER universe, the leader of the angel/demons from the other side known as CENOBITES. Easily identified by his bald head covered in nails, which gave him his name. (In Barker's stories/script, he is never referred to as Pinhead; the make-up effects team coined it and it stuck.) In the feature films, played by Doug Bradley, who gets to say, "I'll tear your soul apart!" and other classic lines later sampled by loads of INDUSTRIAL bands. A most serious villain, whose costume is bound to show up at every Goth HALLOWEEN party 'til the end of time.

PIRATE SHIRT *See: Poet shirt*

PLASTIK WRAP Canadian streetwear clothing company, founded by Adriana Fulop and Ryan Webber in 2001. One of the first to bring futuristic CYBERGOTH designs to North America, specializing in tailored clothes made from high-tech fabrics, with names like "Transform" or "Invader," most suited to dance floors but also appreciated by CORP GOTHS. As befitting a Cyber label, have strong online presence.

PLAY ROOM At a FETISH NIGHT, a space for more sexually explicit activities, often separate and shielded from the main dance floor area.

POE, EDGAR ALLAN American poet, author and literary critic (1809–1849). Truly, no other writer epitomizes so much of what we hold dear. Horror. Romance. Sorrow. A preoccupation with death and returning from death and beautiful women dying and loving dead beautiful women. Humour as black as our souls. Creator of the detective story ("The Murders in the Rue Morgue") and inspiration to later sci-fi writers, Poe mastered tales of mystery and imagination and lived a life as Gothic as his works. Orphaned at a young age when his mother died of tuberculosis, wife killed by the ravages of consumption, descended into a grief-stricken drunk and found delirious and near-death in the wee hours of October 7, 1849, his definite death following a few hours later. The true cause of his demise remains a mystery, as does the identity of the "Poe Toaster," an admirer who visited his grave for more than fifty years on the anniversary of his death. Poe left us a canon that continues to appear in art and popular culture, from the Roger Corman–produced horror films of the 1960s starring VINCENT PRICE, to a never-ending stream of music artists recording their interpretations of his best-known stories and poems. (See, for one example, song versions of his posthumously published "Annabel Lee" by everyone from folk singer Joan Baez to THE CRÜXSHADOWS.) Not to mention, Poe wrote a little something called "THE RAVEN." If there were a citizenship test for Gothdom, reciting some Poe would be it. Buried at Westminster Burial Ground, Baltimore, Maryland.

POET SHIRT Loose-fitting, long-sleeved blouse with many frills at the cuffs and down the front, which is often a low V-shape with laces. Popularized by the NEW ROMANTICS like ADAM ANT and still worn by TRAD GOTHS and ROMANTIGOTHS seeking to project that "I read BYRON" look. Because it's similar to the kind of shirt worn by pirates in movies, sometimes called the pirate shirt. Available in a variety of fabrics from linen to VELVET, it's the one Goth staple that's usually seen in white.

POGS 1. Australian term, short for Post Office Goth, Perth's version of a MALL GOTH. So named because the gothy teens hung out on the steps in front of the General Post Office. 2. Perth Order of Gothic Societies.

POLIDORI, JOHN British writer (1795–1821), author of the first known VAMPIRE story in English, *The Vampyre*. Originally attributed to LORD BYRON, the tale of an aristocratic undead scoundrel launched the romantic vampire fiction genre that we enjoy to this day. Polidori didn't seem to enjoy much: he committed suicide by cyanide poisoning shortly after it was published. His remains are buried at St. Pancras Old Church in London.

POP, IGGY American singer and actor (né James Newell Osterberg Jr., b. April 21, 1947) known as the Grandfather of Punk but plenty Goth too: his wild, confrontational performance (going as far as cutting himself up with broken glass on stage with The Stooges) in the 1960s influencing many, including PETER MURPHY and comic book artist James O'Barr, who modeled Eric "THE CROW" DRAVEN partly after Pop. And he's got the same physique and stamina today, suggesting he just might possibly be an actual VAMPIRE. Even more importantly, his 1977 album *The Idiot* blew minds and was directly responsible for inspiring almost everyone in the early POST-PUNK scene. (They say it was on IAN CURTIS's turntable when his body was found hanged.)

PORNOGRAPHY Fourth studio album by THE CURE, released 1982. The opening lyric is "It doesn't matter if we all die," and it doesn't get any cheerier from there. Dismissed upon its release (*Rolling Stone* called it "adolescent existentialism," as if that were an insult!), now considered the apex of the band's darkest, early days. THE SISTERS and JOY DIVISION be damned, probably the most Goth record of all time.

P. ORRIDGE, GENESIS British musician and artist (né Neil Andrew Megson, b. February 22, 1950) credited with coining the term "INDUSTRIAL music" in 1976, with the formation of Industrial Records by his experimental noise band Throbbing Gristle. As the leader of 1980s psychedelic electronic music/video project Psychic TV, promoted occult magick to the masses through acid house; during the 1990s industrial heyday collaborated with the likes of SKINNY PUPPY. But his greatest artwork is his own existence: a prominent body modifier, he has taken gender bending to new extremes. Starting with breast implants and other plastic surgeries, he ultimately transformed his body into a "pandrogynous" experiment alongside his (late) wife Lady Jaye. Imitable.

POSEUR A pejorative term for a person considered a fake by members of a subculture, from the French verb "to pose." Popularized by punks to describe someone who dresses the part but doesn't listen to the music or understand the culture and used by metal and hip-hop cultures as well. Goths take it even more seriously, devising a variety of words to distinguish and demean different kinds of poseurs. *See also: Doom Cookie, Kindergoth, Mall Goth, NINNY, Mansonite*

POSITIVE PUNK Between punk and POST-PUNK and well before Goth, there was this short-lived term to describe the new black-clad clan. Hard to imagine this dark scene was ever considered positive, but I suppose in contrast to people who used to spit at each other and wear safety pins in their faces for jewelry, it seemed so.

POST-PUNK Musical subgenre that emerged from the British punk rock scene and gave birth to GOTHIC ROCK. Originally coined to describe SIOUXSIE AND THE BANSHEES in *Sounds* magazine in 1977, was soon widely applied to various '80s groups taking punk in a darker, more experimental direction, including BAUHAUS, JOY DIVISION, THE CURE, The Fall, Gang of Four and others. With its emphasis on deep bass, stark, slowed-down rhythms, synthesizers and morbid lyrics — with a very stylish eye towards dress and theatrical live shows — it expressed a different side of musical rebellion, one that resonated across the pond to the NO WAVERS in New York and the DEATH ROCKERS in California. Outgrew itself and split into NEW WAVE, Gothic rock and alternative, with a revival in the 2000s thanks to bands like INTERPOL and others who would never admit to being Goth but will gladly call themselves post-punk.

PRICE, VINCENT American actor (né Vincent Leonard Price Jr., 1911–1993), icon of horror, he of the distinctively low voice and devilish eyebrows and smile. While many children of the 1980s first discovered him from his spoken word on Michael Jackson's hit song "Thriller," Price had been the leading man in scary film and TV since the 1940s, most notably a string of low-budget adaptations of EDGAR ALLAN POE tales in the 1960s including *House of Usher* and *The Masque of the Red Death*. In the 1970s, he appeared on ALICE COOPER's album *Welcome to My Nightmare*, as well as in *The Muppet Show* and Canada's *Hilarious House of Frightenstein*. Price was never famed for one particular role or even style. He could do TV game show humour as well as horror, but he excelled in Gothic and noir pictures, and there was always something delectably macabre about him. A food enthusiast, renowned art collector, fine writer and all around bon vivant, Price is combination Patron Saint and fantasy dad. His final role was in 1990's *EDWARD SCISSORHANDS*, directed by TIM BURTON, a fitting hand-off to the next generation's master of the dark arts. His ashes were scattered at sea.

PROJECT PITCHFORK German SYNTHPOP band formed by Peter Spilles (vocals) and Dirk Scheuber (keyboards) in 1989. Have been adopted by the North American Goth/INDUSTRIAL community, despite the fact they're really neither. Rather, they've brought a new wave of stompy, melodic European-style EBM (sung in English) to these shores that has crossed over into every dark-electro scene. Key tracks: "Souls," "Timekiller."

PROJEKT RECORDS American independent label founded by musician Sam Rosenthal in 1983. Early ads for a free mail-order catalogue summed up its specialty: "ETHEREAL, Gothic, AMBIENT." A counter-point to the California DEATH ROCK scene, Projekt was the home of what came to be known in the later 1990s as "DARKWAVE" (some credit Rosenthal with coining the term), with swirly, more SHOEGAZERY releases by LYCIA, Love Spirals Downwards, Attrition and BLACK TAPE FOR A BLUE GIRL, his own band. Still active, pro-ducing the semi-regular Projektfest music festival and releasing a healthy schedule of enchanting new music.

PROPAGANDA American magazine, edited by Fred Berger in the late 1980s and early '90s. The first North American publication devoted to Goth, and in the pre-internet age the most important source of information and inspiration for those in small towns who managed to stumble upon it through mail or-der (e.g., me!). Initially black and white, heavy on fashion spreads, band interviews and scene reports from L.A., it celebrated all things Goth with an erot-ic eye. Ultimately evolved into a colour mag focused on pictorials of ANDROGYNOUS babes, but not before Berger produced some black-and-white porny Goth videos. Back issues are scarce but well worth collecting.

PSEUDONYM As was so well spoofed by *SNL*'s AZRAEL ABYSS, many Goths like to have names that reflect their true, dark nature. And if you're not fortunate enough to have been named Moon or Raven by your parents, you'll need to come up with your own. This exploded in the internet and role playing–game age, where you'll find no end to the ArcAngels, Baron Von SuchandSuches, Vlad Draculs, Mistress Nightmares and so on. Hey, don't laugh too hard, it was good enough for ANDREW ELDRITCH.

PSYCHIC VAMPIRE *See: Modern vampire*

PSYCHOBILLY *See: Gothabilly*

PUFFY SHIRT What Jerry Seinfeld calls a POET SHIRT. Nobody else does.

PULLING THE TAFFY Sarcastic term for dancing with one's arms reaching up to the rafters and back again in a dramatic fashion. Also known as "Clearing the cobwebs from the attic."

PVC Short for polyvinyl chloride, a plastic material used in fetish wear and other clothing. A little bit spandex, a little bit patent leather, this inexpensive, man-made alternative to animal skins is popular with cheapskates and vegans and anyone looking for that shiny Catwoman/Batman/MATRIX look. The British mods used it for go-go boots and rainslicks in the 1960s, but Goths have helped make a market for PVC everything: pants, skirts, dresses, CORSETS, lingerie, handbags, even T-shirts. Yeah, it might not be the best idea to rub your skin against the same kind of potentially harmful chemicals used to make vinyl siding, but if you're gonna die, might as well die with your shiniest PVC boots on.

QUEEN OF THE DAMNED

QUEEN OF THE DAMNED Horror film directed by Michael Rymer in 2002, based on the epic third novel in ANNE RICE's VAMPIRE Chronicles. Starring Stuart Townsend as the rock star version of Vampire LESTAT, who wakes Akasha, the sexy and sinister "first" vampire, played by R&B singer Aaliyah. A goofier, more adolescent cinematic adaptation of Rice's world than INTERVIEW WITH THE VAMPIRE, with Lestat dressed a bit too much like Eric DRAVEN as THE CROW and a now-dated soundtrack of nü metal, nevertheless it gave a lot of Australian Goth teens roles as extras in the big concert scene. Dedicated to the memory of Aaliyah, who died in 2001 in a plane crash shortly after completing shooting.

RAVEN

RAKS GOTHIQUE *See: Gothic belly dance*

RAMPLING, ANNE Nom de plume for author Anne "Vampire Chronicles" RICE, under which she wrote the sexually provocative novels *Exit to Eden* (1985) and *Belinda* (1986), which explored BDSM and man-girl love, respectively. *See also: Roquelaure, A.N.*

RASPUTINA American cello trio founded by Melora Creager in 1989 as the Travelling Ladies' Cello Society. STEAMPUNK before most Goths even knew what that was, the group combines VICTORIANA with rock 'n' roll, wrapped tightly in CORSETS and a wicked sense of play. The major labels came calling early, and Rasputina enjoyed widespread mainstream promotion in the early '90s, via MARILYN MANSON remixes and placement on *BUFFY THE VAMPIRE SLAYER*. Today, an independent outfit keeping esoteric folk tales alive through DIY recordings and small-scale recitals. Essential tracks: "Transylvanian Concubine," "1816, The Year Without a Summer."

RAVENCROW NEVERSMILES Pseudonym chosen by fictional character Lisa Simpson in the 2004 *Simpsons* episode "Smart and Smarter" when, during an identity crisis, she adopts a Goth persona (after rejecting cheerleader and rapper). Her yellow hair turns black, and she's rocking the FISHNETS. When her nerdy suitor Millhouse mistakes her black-and-purple attire for an Oakland Raiders fan thing, she dismisses him with "It's called Goth, eternally clueless one."

RAVEN, THE Once upon a midnight dreary, real or imagined, EDGAR ALLAN POE wrote this narrative poem about a lovesick young man who goes mad in the presence of a talking raven gently rapping on his chamber door. It was widely published in 1845 and made him famous (if not rich, sadly). In the years since, this well-known verse has become a Goth hymn — memorized, romanticized — and cultural touchstone representing gloominess satirized by everyone from black metal bands to TV comedy writers. An outrageously perfect reading of it by actor Christopher Walken appears on the Poe tribute CD *Closed on Account of Rabies.* When will its impact wane? Obvious: Nevermore.

REACH FOR THE CRYPT One-off Goth game show produced and hosted in 2001 by broadcaster/author/not-so-closet Goth Daniel Richler for Canada's Book Television, in which he quizzed a team (myself included) on DRACULA facts vs. rumour to promote the book *Dracula: Sense and Nonsense* by scholar Elizabeth Miller.

REC.MUSIC.INDUSTRIAL Usenet group formed in 1991 for the discussion of all INDUSTRIAL-related music. For years, an indispensable source of info on new releases and concerts, now mostly a cobweb of its former self. If you have a burning question about the minutiae of Front 242's discography, its old FAQs should be of some assistance.

RECOVERING GOTH An ex-Goth, someone who considers his/her Gothdom to be in the past. Perhaps they don't dress up as much as they used to, or go clubbing anymore. But the fact that they still know enough about the scene to refer to themselves as this in-joke means they are probably still quite Goth on the inside.

REDEMPTION FILMS *See: Salvation Films*

REGULATION COLOURS Acceptable colours for clothing, make-up and home décor. Essentially: black and red. You can also get away with dark purple, burgundy and some shades of green or blue. *See also: Silver*

RELEASE THE BATS 1. Song by The BIRTHDAY PARTY, released 1981. Two-and-a-half minutes of noisy, skronking shrieks! 2. Monthly DEATH ROCK club night held in Long Beach, California, since 1998, featuring live bands and DJs including the event's appropriately named promoter and resident selector Dave Bats. Holding it down for the TRAD GOTHS in the face of Cyber domination for those who like their dancing old school.

REN FAIR Short for Renaissance Fair (sometimes *faire*, *fayre*, etc.), a gathering of enthusiasts of the English Elizabethan era, involving music, food and sports of the period in a festival setting. Attracting a wide range of people, ROMANTIGOTHS in particular love Ren Fairs for the opportunity to wear frilly shirts or CORSETS, polish their swords and hang out with their GOTHLINGS in a family-friendly environment that nurtures their love for history.

RENFIELD 1. Fictional character in BRAM STOKER's *DRACULA* and the cinematic interpretations thereof, a laywer turned lunatic under the spell of Count Dracula who eats spiders and utters the immortal words "The blood is the life!" 2. Renfield's Syndrome, more officially known as clinical vampirism, a mental disorder in which sufferers are obsessed with the drinking of blood.

REPO! THE GENETIC OPERA Horror rock-opera film directed by Darren Lynn Bousman, released 2008, about a future world run amok where organs can be bought — and repossessed. A gory, over-the-top romp that's probably the only movie we'll ever see starring Paris Hilton, Paul Sorvino and OGRE from SKINNY PUPPY together, featuring musical numbers like "Things You See in a Graveyard." Thus, it's developed an underground cult following of "Shadow Casts," who dress up and "Testify!" at screenings, à la *ROCKY HORROR*. A documentary about the fandom by L.A. Goth/horror personality Spooky Dan is in the works.

RE/SEARCH PUBLICATIONS Book and magazine publishing company founded in 1980 by V. Vale, editor of the seminal punk rock fanzine *Search & Destroy*. Devoted to alternative music, film and lifestyle when it was truly underground, its original tabloid zine plus books like MODERN PRIMITIVES and the *Industrial Culture Handbook* have documented with an anthropological and artful eye the greater counter-culture in which Goth exists. Essential reading.

RETAIL SLUT Clothing store on Melrose in Los Angeles opened in 1983 by Helen Bed, a gathering place for punks, Goths, drag queens and other FREAKS until it closed in 2005. Assorted DEATH ROCKERS of note worked there, including ROZZ WILLIAMS and Eva O. of CHRISTIAN DEATH.

REZNOR, TRENT *See: Nine Inch Nails*

RICCI, DONNA American model and clothing designer and one-time self-professed "Gothic Supermodel," she of the ballerina-thin legs and Rapunzel-length hair. Co-creator of the Wicket Talent collective for alternative models. Now designer of STEAMPUNK clothing under the name Clockwork Couture.

RICE, ANNE American author (née Howard Allen O'Brien, b. October 4, 1941), grand dame of the VAMPIRE tale. That one of the bestselling novelists of the twentieth century (100 million books sold and counting) dealt in gloriously Gothic stories of romantic vampire aristocrats warms the cockles of all of our black hearts. During the 1990s, her Vampire Chronicles (INTERVIEW WITH THE VAMPIRE, *Vampire* LESTAT and QUEEN OF THE DAMNED in particular) dominated the book scene, and the films sprung from them fueled our fantasies about New Orleans, decadence and immortality, with later works doing the same for witches. So Rice's announcement in 2005 that she was abandoning the genre, returning to Catholicism and would write henceforth only for the Lord, well, it was a mighty blow. But her canon exists to be savoured eternally, inspiration for all those who want to rule the world by writing stories of love and blood. *See also: Anne Rice Vampire Lestat Fan Club; Louis; Rampling, Anne; Rocquelaure, A.N.*

RIVETHEAD A fan of INDUSTRIAL music, most commonly male, who dresses the part as well as listening to the music. Typical attire is militaristic in nature, often with combat boots, army pants and short/shaved hair in monochromatic black. Accessorizing with more flashy synth dreads, TRANSMUTER boots or GOGGLES has become fashionable in the post-CYBERGOTH age. Although rivetheads and Goths often frequent the same shops and clubs and the term "Industrial Goth" has come into use, the scenes and looks are quite distinct. ANDROGYNY, for one example, is not common in rivetheads. Neither is "PULLING THE TAFFY" or other dramatic arm gestures on the dance floor. Rather, they are more likely to be stomping up a sweat while plotting how "the war for Industrial music must be won!" (Seriously, I saw that graffiti once.) Rivethead girls do exist; they keep the market for TRIPP NYC baggy pants alive.

ROCKY HORROR PICTURE SHOW, THE Horror musical film released in 1975, a parody of B-movies, starring Tim Curry as Dr. Frank-N-Furter, a "sweet transvestite from Transylvania" who looks great in FISHNETS. With its massive cult status for three decades now, it's such a recognizable good-time movie that it provides a great cover for Goth Boys who want cross-dress ("Oh, it's just a *Rocky Horror* costume!") and its signature dance number "Time Warp" gives us something to dance to with our non-Goth family members at weddings.

ROMANTIGOTH The bookish Goths, as interested in the Romantic poets as the NEW ROMANTIC punks, as well as Victoriana, MEDIEVAL history and the like. Typically attired in VELVET, lace and POET SHIRTS, prone to daydreaming and always finding beauty in death and decay. Like the TRAD GOTHS, not too interested in the Cyber scene, but prefer their playlists more on the ETHEREAL and DARKWAVE side rather than sticking with DEATH ROCK. The most likely to organize picnics in cemeteries and know their Beethoven from their Bach.

ROQUELAURE, A.N. Nom de plume for ANNE RICE used for her Sleeping Beauty trilogy, in which she re-imagined the fairytale as an explicit BDSM fantasy. *The Claiming of Sleeping Beauty* (1983), *Beauty's Punishment* (1984) and *Beauty's Release* (1985) actually outsold her *INTERVIEW WITH THE VAMPIRE* novel, which inspired her to write additional pornographic books under the name ANNE RAMPLING. For many who discovered them only after the breakout of the VAMPIRE Chronicles in the early 1990s (by which point her true identity had been revealed), they offered an introduction to the S/M world not generally found on mainstream bookshelves. Censors responded in kind: the Beauty books remain one of the most frequently challenged by libraries and other authorities.

ROSETTA STONE British GOTHIC ROCK band formed by Porl King in 1988, one of the most successful second wave of acts basically re-hashing THE SISTERS/MISSION/ NEFFS formula — right down to the drum machine with its own name (Madame Razor). Nevertheless, thanks to a North American deal with CLEOPATRA RECORDS, and King's openness to communicating directly with his fanbase on Usenet groups in the pre-MySpace age, they found a global audience and a semi-hit with "Adrenaline." After switching to a more INDUSTRIAL sound in the 1990s, they disappeared into the ether forever — declaring at an appearance at WHITBY GOTHIC WEEKEND in 1998 that they were "sick and tired with all the bullshit surrounding the scene."

ROUGH TRADE British record shop, label and distributor, founded by Geoff Travis in 1976, specializing in POST-PUNK. Best known for signing The Smiths (or, to those under thirty, The Strokes), but also home at times to CABARET VOLTAIRE, VIRGIN PRUNES and other important late '70s acts.

RUBBER *See: Latex*

RUE MORGUE Horror magazine and radio show based in Toronto, Canada, founded by Rodrigo Gudiño in 1997, devoted to horror films, art and culture. The *National Geographic* of horror fandom, documenting macabre entertainment and lifestyle in a serious, sexy way that's free of Hollywood-marketing bullshit. As one of its long-time contributors, I believe it's exposing a whole generation of horror movie nerds to great music, books and more that will set them on a darkened path for life. Not a Goth mag per se, but the world is a Gothier place for it.

STOKER

SALEM City in Massachusetts, USA, site of the 1692 witch trials where more than twenty people were killed in a wave of superstition and mass hysteria. Today people go there to buy souvenir broomsticks and magic quartz. Goths who fall into the tourist trap are most often disappointed as it's not really that evil of a place, unless you've got a fear of gift shops.

SALEM'S LOT Novel by STEPHEN KING, published in 1975, about a town in Maine infiltrated by VAMPIREs. With its fog and shadows, foreboding mansion and ghostly child vampire Danny Glick, one of the most traditionally Gothic of modern vampire stories. The 1979 TV miniseries portrays the head vampire as a monstrous, NOSFERATU-like creature, the likes of which are tough to find in the post–ANNE RICE/ TWILIGHT era.

SALVATION GROUP British media company, formed by Nigel Wingrove in 1993, comprising a film distribution company (Redemption), record label (Triple Silence) and magazine (*Nihilista*) specializing in horror and exploitation, especially VAMPIREs and naughty nuns. Famous for its Satanic Sluts, a group of devilishly pervy models/actresses/performance artists who make the SUICIDE GIRLS seem rather sweet.

SAMHAIN 1. Celtic harvest festival of yore, held on October 31, and source of many of our modern HALLOWEEN traditions, such as jack-o-lanterns and costuming. Practiced today by Wiccans and other pagans, and name-dropped by Goths who think it's more authentic than Halloween. 2. Horror punk band, GLENN DANZIG's short-lived project between THE MISFITS and Danzig.

SANCTUARY 1. Online radio station, streaming classic and new Goth/INDUSTRIAL 24/7 at sanctuaryradio .com. 2. Name of the Swiss Gothic Association. 3. Mail-order catalogue created by pop star Cher for a few years in the 1990s, featuring a surprising amount of Gothic home décor — wrought-iron four-poster bed with GARGOYLES anyone? 4. Toronto's Sanctuary Vampire Sex Bar, an all-Goth nightclub operating from 1992 to 2000, which is now a Starbucks; owner Lance Goth (not his real name!) published the collection of short stories *Tales From Sanctuary: The Vampire Sex Bar*.

SANDMAN, THE Comic book series by NEIL GAIMAN, originally published from 1989 to 1996 by DC's Vertigo Press, about MORPHEUS, the King of Dreams, and his siblings Desire, Despair, Destiny, Delirium, Destruction and, most important of all, DEATH. The horror and fantasy worlds created herein were the stuff of real dreams for Goths — villains and heroes in black and PALE white dropping references to Shakespeare and Greek mythology to make us feel smart. A critically acclaimed mainstream blockbuster title, *The Sandman* is probably read by more Goth Girls than every other comic ever made combined, making Gaiman into a icon of the grandest stature.

SAVAGE, JON British music journalist (né Jonathan Sage, b. 1953) who wrote about POST-PUNK and NEW WAVE for *Sounds*, NME and the like, whose 1991 book *England's Dreaming* is the definitive reference for the U.K. punk explosion, including THE DAMNED, SIOUXSIE SIOUX and others.

SCARY LADY SARAH American club DJ and concert promoter from Chicago, now based in Berlin. Resident DJ at Nocturna, Chicago's longest-running Goth/INDUSTRIAL/dark alternative club night, and regular special guest at CONVERGENCE, WAVE-GOTIK-TREFFEN and other major festivals. Known as much for her gravity-defying teased hair as her continued commitment to scouring the underground for new bands to play.

SCHWARZE SZENE German term, literally translates to "black scene" and used since the 1990s to describe all the so-called dark alternative music styles swirling around Goth: INDUSTRIAL, DARKWAVE, electro, metal, neofolk and medieval, and for some reason also including BDSM/fetish culture. Kind of like the Goth version of LGBTTIQQ2SA, but "Schwarze" just sounds so much Gothier. Not widely used outside of Germany.

SCREAM Los Angeles nightclub and live music venue, operated by Bruce Perdew and Michael Stewart at the Embassy Hotel from 1989 to 1999. A massive, multi-level space with a "Stairway to Hell" up to the dark dance floor, where FREAKS of all ages and persuasions would gather late into the night/morning, but none so purposefully as the DEATH ROCKERS, who made it their after-hours home. *See also: Helter Skelter*

SDAM Singapore Dark Alternative Movement, organization started in 1998 by Saito Nagasaki to put on Goth events and promote the subculture throughout the country.

SECRET GOTH CABAL Can't talk about this. Sorry.

SEX Clothing boutique located at 430 King's Road in Chelsea, London, operated by punk impresario Malcolm McLaren and designer VIVIENNE WESTWOOD from 1974 to 1976. (Previously known as rock shop Paradise Garage and Teddy Boy outfitters Let It Rock.) Sold LATEX/fetish/bondage wear and incorporated that scene's studs and zippers and such to original Westwood designs, particularly her sometimes pornographic, always provocative T-shirts that helped define the distressed punk rock style. Changed names a few times and closed for good in 1980.

SEXBAT Pseudonym for one of the co-founders of ALT.GOTHIC, who is credited with coining the term NET.GOTH.

SEX GANG CHILDREN British POST-PUNK group lead by singer Andi Sex Gang (né Andreas McElligott) formed in 1981, part of the original BATCAVE crew. Andi's upper-range vocals proved you don't need to be baritone to be Goth. In fact, at least one person (IAN ASTBURY) claims the origin of the G-word is his nicknaming the short-statured, hyperactive Andi, who lived in a place called Visigoth Towers, the "Gothic Goblin." Drama followed the band on stage and off, and they never quite got their due before splitting in 1984; the DEATH ROCK revival has put them back in the spotlight and they now headline Goth festivals in Europe. A documentary about Andi, *Bastard Art*, was released in 2009.

SHELLEY 1. Mary Shelley (née Mary Wollstonecraft Godwin, 1797–1851), British writer, author of *FRANKENSTEIN*. Writing the world's great monster story earned her a place in literary history, but the fact that she kept the actual heart of her late-husband Percy (rescued from the funeral pyre by a friend), wrapped in the pages of his elegiac poem *Adonaïs* also makes her the godmother of ROMANTIGOTHS everywhere. Buried at St. Peter's Church in Dorset, ENGLAND. 2. Percy Bysshe Shelley (1792–1822), Mary's husband, one of the great Romantic poets. Chastised in his time by those who knew him for being a political reformer and atheist, remembered now for his Gothic novels, lovely lyrical verse and the essay *A Defense of Poetry* (which, to Goths, needs no defense at all). Bonus points for being able to correctly spell his middle name. Drowned at sea, his cremated remains (sans heart) are in a cemetery in Rome.

SHOEGAZER Musical subgenre practiced by some U.K. rock groups in the mid to late 1980s, so called for a tendency for the musicians to spend the entire show gazing at their shoes. They were more likely looking down at their pedals — the genre is defined by a wash of guitar effects and other droning, psychedelic noises coupled with processed, melodic vocals. Although most shoegazers were not Goth (those were sneakers they were staring at, after all), it did start with the COCTEAU TWINS and we probably wouldn't have ETHE-REAL without it.

SIDE-LINE Webzine dedicated to the darkest side of independent electronic music (i.e., INDUSTRIAL and its various descendents), started as a French-language print magazine in 1989 by David Noiret and Seba Dolimont now operating as an excellent source of music news online, with an active forum where RIVET-HEADS can get their old school NET.GOTH geek on.

SIGUE SIGUE SPUTNIK British glam punk outfit formed in 1982 by bassist Tony James (ex–Generation X, future SISTERS OF MERCY) best remembered for the club single "Love Missile F1-11" and selling adverts between the tracks of their debut album, *Flaunt It*. Jones has described SSS as "hi-tech sex, designer violence and the fifth generation of rock 'n' roll," but with their massive neon hairdos and a heavy metal meets sci-fi fashion sense that back then was outrageous even by Japanese standards, they may very well have been the world's first CYBERGOTHS.

SIGUSMONDI, FLORIA Canadian photographer and filmmaker (b. 1965), whose freakish, hyper-kinetic, gorgeously grotesque style established in "The Beautiful People" music video for MARILYN MANSON has been ripped off by thousands of people who want to look dark and "edgy."

SIOUXSIE AND THE BANSHEES British POST-PUNK group formed 1976 by vocalist SIOUXSIE SIOUX and bassist Steven Severin. From their very first gig (featuring the future Sid Vicious on drums) improvising noise over the Lord's Prayer, they carved a new path out of punk, incorporating both pop and the avant garde. Eschewing the straight-up B-movie macabre of their contemporaries, they created instead psychedelic dreamworlds of magic and sensuality, with horror coming in unexpected places — like 1984's "Cities in Dust," an ode to the destroyed city of Pompeii with lyrics about hot lava pouring into gaping mouths. They split in 1996; a 2004 box set, *Downside Up*, collects their best work.

SIOUX, SIOUXSIE British singer (née Susan Janet Ballion, b. May 27, 1957), leader of the Banshees and THE CREATURES and a style icon who gave Goth Girls the idea for their BACKCOMBED black hair and Cleopatra eye make-up look. But we should not reduce all of her efforts down to that one iconic image: as a fiercely assertive artist who pushed boundaries even within the punk scene (wearing a swastika, for one), and writer of some of the great pop hits of the 1980s, she has inspired in many ways. And her vocal style is beyond compare. A 2007 solo album, *Mantaray*, full of electro-pop-rock glamour, proved she's still vital, ageless.

SISTERHOOD, THE A legal pissing contest disguised as band. This short-lived project for THE SISTERS OF MERCY singer ANDREW ELDRITCH released only one single ("Giving Ground") and one album (*Gift*) in 1985–1986 as a way to stop his ex-bandmates WAYNE HUSSEY and Craig Adams from using the name themselves or collecting publishing money due to the group. Stripped of guitars, the songs were constructed with unsophisticated drum machine rhythms and guest vocalists doing their faux Eldritch best — not particularly well received by the press but they are gloriously gloomy, brazenly unconventional for the time and can still pack a dance floor today. They did not, as Eldritch has implied, inspire the techno movement.

SISTERS OF MERCY, THE British rock band, formed 1980 by singer ANDREW ELDRITCH and guitarist Gary Marx and featuring various members including WAYNE HUSSEY and Craig Adams, later of THE MISSION. Note that I didn't use "GOTHIC ROCK" band. Because ever since the Sisters invented Gothic rock, Eldritch has been denying it. One can't blame the man for disassociating himself from a style that also was used to describe The Mission and hundreds of uninspired copycats thereof, and it's true that they stretched beyond the style over the years, from ambient to full-on metal, but the hard truth is that there is none more Goth than the Sisters. Their three early singles and three studio albums are gospel, even their current live incarnation (Eldritch + some unknown musicians nobody cares about + tons and tons of fog) fly the tattered flag of doom-obsessed dirges that sing this corrosion and dance the ghost all over the black planet, black world of Gothdom.

SILVER Metal of choice for jewels and accessories. Perhaps because it's associated with the moon rather than the golden sun. Or perhaps because it's cheaper. Either way, it goes well with black.

SKELLINGTON, JACK Fictional Pumpkin King star of TIM BURTON's animated *NIGHTMARE BEFORE CHRISTMAS* feature. Tall and, um, skeletal, in his pinstriped suit and BAT-shaped bowtie, he's the hero of HALLOWEEN Town and our hearts.

SKINNY PUPPY Canadian industrial group, formed in Vancouver in 1982 by cEvin Key and NIVEK OGRE. Pioneers of a danceable evolution of European-style avant garde electronic noise layered with sinister horror movie samples and disturbing, distorted vocals, often with a political sloganeering bent. If that sounds like rather standard fare for INDUSTRIAL now, remember that it wasn't in the 1980s: it's Skinny Puppy who popularized industrial music in North America back then, also drenching it with gory, GRAND GUIGNOL visual presentation that perfected the long simmering Goth/industrial fusion. Had a tragic end in 1995, when long-time member Dwayne Goettel died of a drug overdose while a tension-plagued recording of the big-budget album *The Process* tore them apart. In their absence, Ministry and NINE INCH NAILS grabbed the industrial baton and ran with it to the top of the MTV charts, but Puppy was there first. In 2000, band reunited for the Doomsday Festival, so the next generation of Goths could see how it's done. Key tracks: "Dig It," "Testure," "Worlock," "Killing Game."

SKIN TWO British fetish empire, founded by Tim Woodward and Grace Lau in 1983 as a club night, followed by a magazine, now includes a clothing line. Their appreciation of LATEX clothing in particular has led to the annual Rubber Ball, the world's largest.

SLIMELIGHT London nightclub, billed as the world's longest-running Goth club, running every Saturday until the morning light. Started in the early 1980s in some small seedy venues (hence the name) now located in the cavernous Elektrowerkz (a paintball venue by day!). Several floors, lots of fog, more hard and heavy EBM, noise and other non-rock music than you'll find at most clubs, which makes for a diverse crowd from ROMANTIGOTHS to RIVETHEADS. Distinguished by its strict members-only policy and dress code, which explicitly states no jeans or sneakers. A sanctuary from the MUNDANE.

SMITH, ROBERT British singer and guitarist (b. April 21, 1959), Our Leader of THE CURE. Smearer of red lipstick, teaser of hair, writer of love songs and lover of cats, Smith is the softer side of Goth rockstardom, dressed in black and wallowing in gloom, certainly, but with a rather pleasant, non-confrontational disposition. He even married his teenage sweetheart. Also displays a fine sense of humour: see him guest star in a *South Park* episode as a giant moth monster battling Barbra Streisand. Bob, however far away, whatever words you say, we will always love you.

SNAKEBITE A beer cocktail of sorts made by combining lager and cider. Obviously, it's a U.K. thing, popular with Goths in pubs. The addition a shot of black currant liquer makes it a Snakebite and Black. A shot of pernod makes it a Red Witch.

SONIC SEDUCER German music magazine, founded 1995, edited by Thomas Vogel, focused on Goth/ INDUSTRIAL and metal music. Sometimes packaged with a CD or DVD compilation of new music.

SOPOR AETERNUS AND THE ENSEMBLE OF SHADOWS

German ÜBERGOTH group, founded in 1989 and led by Anna-Varney Cantodea, a transgendered goddess of night. Sometimes modern SYNTHPOP, sometimes olde world MEDIEVAL, the music sounds a lot like the album titles suggest it would: e.g., debut release . . . *Ich töte mich jedesmal aufs Neue, doch ich bin unsterblich, und ich erstehe wieder auf; in einer Vision des Untergangs* . . . (seriously, it reportedly translates to "I kill myself every time again, but I am immortal, and I rise again; in a vision of Doom"). Cantodea is ever elusive and reclusive, never performing live, appearing instead in dramatic black-and-white photographs and videos designed for maximum ambiguity, and yet she exhibits humanity and humour in her blog posts and communications with fans. If GENESIS P. ORRIDGE took over vocal duties for CHRISTIAN DEATH, it might look and sound something like this.

SOUNDS British music magazine, published from 1970 to 1991. Most associated with the New Wave of British Heavy Metal but did give the POST-PUNKERS some ink. Some say they coined the G-word in a February 1981 feature about the band U.K. Decay called "The Face of Punk Gothique."

SPECIMEN British BATCAVE band formed in 1980 by singer Ollie Wisdom, who ran the Batcave club and helped make Specimen its house band. The group managed a few songs and the EP *Batastrophe* before splitting in 1985, but left a legacy in the image of keyboardist Jonny Slut, he of the famous DEATHHAWK. A 2008 reunion for the club's twenty-fifth anniversary was recorded and released as *Specimen Alive at the Batcave*. Key track: "Kiss, Kiss, Bang, Bang."

SPF 1000 The highest (imaginary) Sun Protection Factor in sunscreen for blacking out UV-B rays. Goths are incredibly crafty at sourcing the highest SPF products, and while SPF 50 will usually suffice, when we joke about a 1000+ SPF, we're only half joking. A Gothic metal band has adopted the name.

SPIDERWEB In nature, the sticky trap spun by spiders with their silk, usually in an orbital shape, to catch prey. In Gothdom, a pretty pattern made with lace, string, beads or drawn in pen or EYELINER that mimics the typical spiderweb shape, used in clothing and jewelry design, home décor and make-up application. The spiderweb follows the skull and the BAT as telltale signifiers of Goth. There are even spiderweb-inspired wedding gowns. Being Goth doesn't mean natural talent at creating a good web: I would enter as evidence the pitiful spiderweb I once made from yarn and hung in my first apartment, but my then-roommate wisely disposed of it.

SPOOKY KIDS Fans of MARILYN MANSON, so named after his first incarnation of the band, called Marilyn Manson and the Spooky Kids. No longer widely used. *Compare: Mansonite*

STAKE Sharpened instrument of wood or other material, often used for nefarious purposes, such as burning witches or impaling adulterers or killing VAMPIRES. So not the right housewarming gift for Goths, then.

STARKERS CORSET and clothing design company, founded by Dianna DiNoble in 1992. Specializing in custom steel-boned corsets based on historical designs, popular with brides.

STEAMPUNK Literary movement combining elements of sci-fi and history to re-envision the steam-powered era with modern or fantasy technological advancements. Originating in the 1980s, it picked up, um, steam (I know, I know, groan) in the early 2000s. And if it's fun to imagine and write about such a thing, it's even more fun to bring it to life with costumes and other objects modified to give them a VICTORIAN-Cyber make-over. Hence, Goths have flocked to the Steampunk scene in their reconstructed CORSETS, custom leather and brass aviator GOGGLES and spats, enjoying an alternative to similarly styled but dystopian CYBERGOTH that lets them geek out over the mechanics of clocks and philosophize a more positive outlook for the future. For Steampunkers, brown is the new black.

STEELE, PETER American singer and musician (né Petrus Ratajczyk, 1962–2010), leader of GOTHIC METAL band TYPE O NEGATIVE. Steele immortalized Goth Girls in the song "BLACK NO. 1 (Little Miss Scare All)," and made quite a few of them happy with his *Playgirl* centerfold in 1995, for which he insisted on appearing erect. For all the DEATH ROCK singers who paint their faces ghoulishly and crawl out of COFFINS, this hulking, arrogant, black-haired baritone was the closet thing to a real VAMPIRE rock star we had. He died of heart failure and is buried at Saint Charles Cemetery in Farmingdale, New York.

STEEL TOE Boot with a steel reinforcement in the toe, made by DOC MARTEN and others. Great for not getting your feet crushed in a crowded concert. A bitch at airport security.

STIFF RECORDS British record label associated with punk and NEW WAVE, formed 1976 by Dave Robinson and Andrew Jakeman. Released THE DAMNED debut "New Rose" on 7", widely considered to be the first punk rock record. Self-proclaimed "undertakers to the industry."

STOKER, BRAM Irish writer (1847–1912), author of *DRACULA*. While Stoker also wrote other tales of Gothic horror, such as *The Lair of the White Worm* and the short story "Dracula's Guest," and was a theatre critic and the business manger of the Lyceum, he is immortal for penning the most influential VAMPIRE tale in history.

SUICIDE GIRLS Website and media empire built on pin-ups and softcore porn photos of alternative models, including Goths and punks and girls with freakishly coloured hair, piercings and TATTOOS, launched in 2001 by Sean Suhl and Selena "Missy Suicide" Mooney. A controversial enterprise: on the one hand, exhibitionist women of an alternative style have a place to strut their stuff and build a profile. On the other hand, SG gives off the impression that all freaky looking girls are slutty. Also, they're pretty much all white and skinny and blemish-free — not all that alternative if you ask me. You might find loads of raven-haired beauties on SG, but actual Goths are few and far between.

SUNGLASSES Don't leave home without them.

SWAMPIE Australian Goths of a certain persuasion ("existentialist, alternative-theatre" types who listen to NICK CAVE and Tom Waits, apparently) in the early 1990s. No longer in widespread use.

SWEEPING THE FLOOR Dance move in which girls (or boys) wearing elaborate gowns appear to be sweeping the floor with their flowing shirt sleeves, done by dramatically swishing the arms while keeping them close to the body.

SWITCHBLADE SYMPHONY American SYNTHPOP group formed in 1989 by Susan Wallace and Tina Root. Taking a big striped tight—clad step away from THE SISTERS—derived DEATH ROCK of the day, the PERKY GOTH duo combined trip-hop beats with ETHEREAL vocals and fairytale-like lyrics. Colourful costumes (including big dreadlocks years before the CYBERS would make it de rigeur) and theatrical productions helped them stand out even further on the CLEOPATRA RECORDS roster. Only managed three albums before splitting in 1999. Hits include "Dissolve" and "Clown."

SWOONING To faint from sheer rapture. An activity long overlooked by the modern man and woman, yet practiced unabashedly by the Goths, usually in the presence of PETER MURPHY or a particularly beautiful full moon.

SYNTHDREADS Synthetic dreadlocks, commonly worn by CYBERGOTHS as temporary ponytail extensions in superbright colours, called FALLS. Can also be affixed more permanently but the idea is to bypass the commitment and hair damage of actual dreads while still enjoying their bad-ass-ness.

SYNTHPOP Musical genre born in the 1970s and popularized in the 1980s where synthesizers are the predominant instrument, pop hooks rule and Kraftwerk shall be worshipped as the robot overlords they are. A precursor to NEW WAVE, the best example of which is Depeche Mode. Electro-obsessed Goth acts continue to practice and it's often listed alongside NEW WAVE, EBM and DARKWAVE on event posters but it's difficult to draw a distinguishing line. How about, bands who are cheerier than darkwave and more retro than futurepop are synthpop?

TRANSMUTER

TAMAGOTHI Online parody of the Tamagotchi virtual pet toy craze, created in 1997 by programmer R. Hunter Gough. In his crudely drawn Shockwave game/site (the Tamagothi never existed in real life), your skull egg would hatch into a BattyGothi then, depending on how well you denied it love and sunlight, would grow into a MopeyGothi, RomantiGothi, IndustrialGothi or, the ultimate success, the MurphyGothi. In a way, the NET.GOTH version of THE MUNSTERS.

TATTOOS As with pretty much every modern subculture at this point, tattoos are acceptable and widespread in Gothdom. And as with pretty much every person tattooed, Goths choose designs based on individual interests, from dainty to crude to entire full-colour sleeves. Some common themes include tribal or Celtic swirls, monsters from favourite horror films, faeries, band logos (NIN and Neubauten symbols lend themselves nicely), all manner of skulls and perhaps the greatest Goth symbol: a BAT. Massive tattooing is not necessarily a sign of GOTHER THAN THOU-ness. Most keep them covered, although extreme or visible tattoos are certainly no taboo. *See also: Modern primitives*

TEMPLE OF LOVE Song by THE SISTERS OF MERCY, originally released as a non-album track in 1983 and re-recorded in 1992 with guest vocalist Ofra Haza for the greatest hits compilation *Some Girls Wander by Mistake.* In either version, the definitive Goth dance floor anthem, a full-blown epic of melodramatic doom that is at once disco and heavy metal and GOTHIC ROCK, made even better by the seven-minute-plus extended remixes the DJ puts on when he/she needs to run to the washroom. The song every devil in a black dress will request 'til the end of time.

TEPES, VLAD Romanian prince (1431–1476) more commonly known as Vlad the Impaler, widely considered the source of inspiration for BRAM STOKER's *DRACULA*, and thus, one of the few historical characters every Goth pretends to know something about. While Stoker did name his Count for Vlad's other family name, Dracul, how much he knew of Vlad's life — particularly his battle victories and taste for impaling his victims — is open to debate. This hasn't kept storytellers from drawing a connection for decades (most notably Francis Ford Coppola for his Dracula flick), to the point where historical sites tied to his life are now marketed to VAMPIRE fans, and many a Goth Boy has used "Vlad" as a pseudonym.

TONES ON TAIL British pop group, a short-lived side-project for guitarist DANIEL ASH in the wake of BAUHAUS's split, also featuring Bauhaus roadie Glenn Campling and Bauhaus drummer KEVIN HASKINS. Between 1982 and 1984, it packed a dizzying variety of styles into its few releases, from AMBIENT synth to neo prog to full-on GOTHIC ROCK. Best known for its heavily sampled/licensed 1984 hit single "Go!," the only tune sure to get Goths skanking on the dance floor. *See also: Love and Rockets*

TOP HAT Fancy hat, tall, brimmed and with a flat top. Historically, an upper crust opera accessory for men, but today's ROMANTIGOTHS and STEAMPUNKS, both male and female, wear them. Miniature top hats, sometimes decorated with lace and ribbons, are popular with GOTHIC LOLITAS.

TOP OF THE POPS British TV show, featuring live (well, lip synched) performances of songs on the U.K. charts, on the air from 1964 to 2006. Amazingly, most of the early Goths had the hits to appear: THE DAMNED, SIOUXSIE, ADAM ANT, THE CURE (seek out their 1980 performance of "A Forest" for some choice footage of ROBERT SMITH pre—FAT BOB hairdo). Strangest moment: NICK CAVE playing backdrop for Kylie Minogue in their murder ballad duet "Where the Wild Roses Grow."

TORTURE GARDEN London fetish club, operating monthly events since 1990, now billed as the world's largest fetish gathering. Certainly the most famous for enthusiasts of high fantasy fashion, extreme body performance art and other more hardcore pursuits than found at your standard Goth fet night. While catering to a diverse crowd with a variety of music, its roots are squarely in the early INDUSTRIAL/noise scene. Its dress code states: if it wouldn't get you stared at on the street, don't wear it to Torture Garden. Amen!

TRAD GOTH What the hip-hoppers would call Old School. Someone who listens to the original GOTHIC ROCK and POST-PUNK bands of the '70s and '80s and dresses the part: pointy shoes, VELVET CLOAKS, ripped FISHNETS, etc. None of that INDUSTRIAL music or neon SYNTHDREADS for the Trad Goth! There is no sense of GOTHER THAN THOU—ness for this choice, although they are proud of it. What the general public would recognize as a Goth is most likely a Trad Goth.

TRANSMUTER Boots created by Brit Terry de Havilland in the early 2000s that boast extreme height and customizable heels and tongues. You buy one style (usually the knee-high black five-inch platforms) and add on whatever you like: SILVER chrome plates, purple SPIDERWEBS, studs, etc. Extremely popular with CYBERGOTHS for that extreme sci-fi look and with short rock stars like MARILYN MANSON and Gene Simmons, as such sneered at by some TRAD GOTHS as a sign of the apocalypse. No longer manufactured but knock-offs are widely available.

TRANSYLVANIA Historical region of Romania, traditional home of fictional VAMPIRES since BRAM STOKER set his DRACULA novel there. It is indeed full of MEDIEVAL castles, was once ruled by the Visigoths, and sounds devilish. So while no modern Goth scene has sprung up from there, most of us do hope to visit someday. Meanwhile, we enjoy its appearances in books and magazines, most notably ROCKY HORROR and the best Bugs Bunny short ever, "Transylvania 6-5000." Abraca-pocus!

TRASH AND VAUDEVILLE NYC clothing store, the epicenter of punk and goth shopping in the Big Apple since 1975. No matter your subgenre or style you can be outfitted here from head to toe: sneakers, stilettos, DOCS, leopard-print skinny jeans, POET SHIRTS, LATEX CORSETS, VELVET gowns, T-shirts, day-glo wigs, BAT necklaces, motorcycle jackets and on and on. Shopping at these two shops — one up an iron staircase, the other down below — on St. Mark's Place is a rite of passage, a pilgrimage, an authentic experience made all the crazier by a run-in with resident staffer Jimmy Webb. No online store, no franchising, no cheap skull-adorned plastic shit from China, just original punk rock attitude all the way.

TRENCHCOAT MAFIA Non-existent Goth gang invented by hysterical media in the wake of the COLUMBINE high school massacre, after it was rumoured that the two killers belonged to a school clique with that name which was associated with MARILYN MANSON and therefore Goths. In truth, there was a small group of like-minded gamers, some of whom wore trenchcoats, who were dubbed that by Columbine jocks, who then reclaimed it for themselves. While it eventually came out that the killers were not part of any Trenchcoat Mafia, some schools actually did ban the coats. Even today, Goth high school kids not looking to arouse suspicions keep theirs at home.

TRIBAL A modern style of belly dance popular with Goths. *See also: Gothic belly dance*

TRINITY Character in THE MATRIX films, played by Carrie-Anne Moss. A computer hacker with bad-ass martial arts and motorcycle driving skills, she has done more to popularize the skin-tight, shiny black catsuit look than anyone since Michelle Pfeiffer's Catwoman. Doesn't need neon hair: totally CYBERGOTH.

TRIPP NYC Clothing label founded by Daang Goodman in 1984, specializing in rock 'n' roll denim; its blood-spattered or razor-blade ripped skinny jeans are the classics, but it was the oversized, wide-legged bondage-strap pants with neon accents that were all the rave for RIVETHEADS and CYBERGOTHS in the late 1990s.

TRUE BLOOD TV supernatural drama based on the Southern VAMPIRE Mysteries book series by Charlaine Harris. No actual Goths on the show, but as Gothic as it gets: sex and violence in the Louisiana heat; vamps and shapeshifters and voodoo and psychics; a bar called Fangtasia, even! And plenty of blood for would-be "Fangbangers." Harris and the show's creator Alan Ball have crafted the best vampire TV since DARK SHADOWS, good enough to shell out $10 a bottle for their *True Blood*–branded blood orange soda, the new straight-edge Goth cocktail of choice.

TUBULAR CRIN *See: Cyberlox*

TWILIGHT Since the 2008 blockbuster film, the bane of our existence. For the record, people: real VAMPIRES don't sparkle. Now, for bringing a whole new generation over to the dark side with her vampire romance empire, author Stephenie Meyer deserves some GOTH POINTS. It really is too bad the whole thing is basically about abstinence. And sparkling.

TYPE O NEGATIVE American GOTHIC METAL band, formed in Brooklyn in 1989 and led by the hulking, ÜBERGOTH baritone/bassist PETER STEELE. Dubbed the "Drab Four" for their doomy sound and macabre lyrics, as exhibited on the hit album *Bloody Kisses*, they brought MUNSTERS-style black humour back from the dead and legions of HOT TOPIC shoppers lined up to worship them. Following the death of Steele in April 2010, fate is uncertain. *See also: Black No. 1*

ÜBERGOTH

ÜBERGOTH Most definitely, excessively, exquisitely Goth. The epitome of Gothness. One who radiates darkness, breathes despair, bleeds black. Or someone who goes out dressed to the nines in full-on TRANSMUTERS and PVC and whiteface to get bread from the corner store. Used good-naturedly to describe anyone who is just seen as very, very, very Goth all the time. Can also be used to describe a temporary state or action that is very, very, very Goth ("CLOVE cigarettes? How übergoth of you!"). The prefix über can also be used alone to express the excessive Gothness of any person, place or thing ("That VELVET HOBBLESKIRT is totally über"); the "Goth" part is understood. How this German term came to be widely used to describe anything extremely Goth is unknown, but points to a longstanding fascination with all things Deutsch, a country which, of course, is totally über.

UNCLE NEMESIS British writer and concert promoter (né Michael Johnson), who organized concerts and events under the name Nemesis Promotions from 1995 to 2001. Now runs the website Nemesis to Go, where he continues to review new bands and their live shows.

URBAN DECAY American cosmetics company founded in 1996 by Sandy Lerner, who, frustrated at the lack of purple nail polish, created her own. Then came the black lipstick (Oil Slick), the green eyeshadows (Acid Rain) and soon a whole range of non-traditional colours trumpeted under the ad slogan "Does pink make you puke?" You might not think Goths need anything more than black EYELINER to be happy, but for everyone who craves an eye-popping shade or the ultimate glitter (many of them vegan friendly too), Urban Decay has become the go-to make-up line.

URBAN GOTHIC British horror TV series focused on seedy or supernatural tales from the London underground. Short-lived (2000–2001) and low budget, but it did a decent job of putting teenage necromancy and vampirism on the telly, even getting scream queen Ingrid Pitt to make an appearance. Available on DVD.

VAMPIRE DISPATCHING KIT

VAMP 1. A femme fatale type, the kind of woman who uses sex as a weapon. All female VAMPIRES are vamps but not all vamps are vampires. And not all Goths are either. Pretty much only used by boys who watch a lot of film noir. 2. Horror comedy from 1986 starring singer Grace Jones as the vampire queen Katrina, featuring one of the freakiest vamp dance sequences ever committed to celluloid.

VAMPIRA American television personality created by actress Maila Nurmi (1922–2008), based on the Charles Addams cartoon character of MORTICIA. As the host of *The Vampira Show* in the 1950s, she set the template for campy, sexed-up femme fatales, with her look of skin-tight black dress, long black hair, exaggerated eyebrows, black fingernails, extremely corseted waist, trademark goofy graveyard puns and piercing scream. Some say she put a curse on her friend James Dean, but she was no witch, just a really great actress. Her horror hostess style was resurrected in the 1980s by Cassandra Peterson as ELVIRA, and although the two fought legal battles over the rights to that image, Goth Girls know the difference and love 'em both. Nurmi's remains rest at the Hollywood Forever Cemetery.

VAMPIRE Mythological bloodsuckers, the Goth's favourite horror movie villain, standard HALLOWEEN costume, dream date. For those people who think they're real, see MODERN VAMPIRES.

VAMPIRE BATS BATS that feed on blood, hunting unsuspecting mammals in the night. Biologists call them *Desmodus rotundus*, *Diphylla ecaudata* and *Diaemus youngil*; Goths dream of them transforming into a human VAMPIRE, like they do in books. If only.

VAMPIRE DISPATCHING KIT Mythical antique object, also known as a VAMPIRE Killing Kit, allegedly made in the nineteenth-century to take care of the pesky NOS-FERATU problem, now sold to rich Goths looking for a real piece of vampire history. Except they're probably fake — a beautiful antique wooden box filled with dusty prayer books, holy water vials, daggers and STAKES, now worth ten times its value for the fancy marketing. Better to buy a contemporary replica. Plus, if the real vampires attack, do you really want to depend on a used one?

VAMPIREFREAKS Social networking site exclusively for Goth/INDUSTRIAL types (or other "tormented souls" and "beautiful FREAKS") created by RIVETHEAD computer programmer Jethro Berelson in 1999, now boasting more than two million users. Like MySpace, LiveJournal, iTunes and Craiglist rolled into one, it's a one-stop virtual shop for Goth living. BABYBATS in particular have flocked to it to create profiles and make spooky love connections in an unfettered environment where they feel free to expresses their innermost pain. Problem is: nobody's moderating or monitoring all these underagers, and the site has been tainted by several high profile, serious crimes by its members, including rape and murder. Most adult Goths find the site either ridiculous or disturbing or both.

VAMPIRE'S ANKH *See: Ankh*

VAMPIRE: THE MASQUERADE Role-playing game developed by White Wolf Publishing. For those who really, really want to create their own VAMPIRE alter ego, join a clan and act out their fantasies in a safe, fun environment. Participation exploded in the 1990s, spinning off into books and even a short-lived TV series, *Kindred: The Embraced*. *See also: LARP*

VAMPYRE SOCIETY British organization for VAMPIRE enthusiasts, active in the 1990s. Not the MODERN VAMPIRES who believe they are undead; rather, people who like graveyard tea parties and Gothic horror novels (i.e., Goths). Turned into a similar group called Vampyre Connexions in 1998 but now seems to be defunct.

V & A The Victorian and Albert Museum in London, home to 4.5 million objects of decorative arts and design. Admirers of MEDIEVAL, VICTORIAN, Elizabethan

275

and Renaissance eras (i.e., % 90 of Goths) will swoon at its extensive collection of decadent textiles, furniture, jewels, sculpture and more. Yes, it has some of the world's most famous stained glass, CANDELABRAS, reliquaries, CORSETS and the like, from such Gothic luminaries as Horace Walpole, William Morris and VIVIENNE WESTWOOD, but it's the sum total, and the glorious building itself, all wrought iron and mosaic tiles, that make it site of Goth pilgrimage. The 2003 exhibition Gothic Art for ENGLAND can still be enjoyed in book form.

VANIAN, DAVE British singer (né David Lett, b. October 12, 1956), leader of THE DAMNED. Ex-gravedigger and horror film fan, he took his stage name to rhyme with Transylvanian, used COFFINS as concert props, wore ghoulish make-up and streaked his hair black and white and generally indulged in macabre presentation well before BATCAVE and GOTHIC ROCK were ever born. So while PETER MURPHY may be the Godfather of Goth, Vanian is its actual dad. Also leads PSYCHOBILLY band David Vanian and the Phantom Chords and is married to PATRICIA MORRISON, ex–SISTERS OF MERCY.

VARNEY THE VAMPIRE British horror serial about a cursed bloodsucker, Sir Francis Varney, written by James Malcolm Rymer and published as a series of cheap penny dreadfuls in the 1840s. Pure VICTORIAN Gothic VAMPIRE fiction, which established such well-known tropes as FANGS, hypnotism and superpowers.

VELVET Fabric of kings and queens and MEDIEVAL times, soft yet heavy, luxurious to the touch; no TRAD GOTH wardrobe is complete without a velvet CLOAK or gown or TOP HAT.

VICIOUS, LIZ American porn actress of a Goth persuasion. If you're into that, just Google her.

VICTORIAN The era of Alexandrina Victoria, Queen of ENGLAND (roughly 1837–1901), romanticized by the ROMANTIGOTHS and the STEAMPUNKS for its ornate architecture (indeed, the Gothic Revival starts here); its abundance of lace and fanciful dress, CORSETS and waistcoats; its perceived majesty of living.

VIRGIN PRUNES Irish POST-PUNK group formed in 1977 that frankly, was GOTHER THAN THOU, or me, or most of the BATCAVERS of the 1980s. Not just for the unsettling, horror-drenched sounds on albums like . . . *If I Die, I Die* and songs like "Baby Turns Blue" but for the brazen theatricality of their live shows, GRAND GUIGNOL in miniature, with PALE white faces in cross-dress, enshrouded in fog, simulating sodomy and other acts of deviant decadence — in Ireland! In the 1970s! So sadly short lived, and never big in America. Look 'em up.

VISUAL KEI Japanese music style associated with GOTHIC LOLITA scene. Like glam metal mating with cyberpunk in a historical VICTORIAN manga, visual kei artists flaunt ANDROGYNY, colour and frills in a way that no Western artist could ever get away with. Hence, most of us have never heard of it, but if you're wondering where over-the-top creative costuming in pop music went, look to the East. *See also: Mana*

VODKA-CRAN Vodka and cranberry, the Goth cocktail of choice.

VOLTAIRE 1. American musician, writer, animator and comic book artist (né Aurelio Voltaire Hernandez, b. January 25, 1967), best known for his graphic novel *Oh My Goth!* and the humourous and handy guidebooks *What Is Goth?* and *Paint It Black: A Guide to Gothic Homemaking.* He spins a fine goth folk song too, tongue always firmly in cheek, and has released several albums on PROJEKT RECORDS. In addition to singing in night-clubs, you can find it him in animated form in the game *Adventure Quest World*, at comic conventions plugging his Deady Bear line of gruesome toy collectibles or just enjoying a good laugh at his own expense. 2. Pen name for seventeenth-century French writer/ philosopher François-Marie Arouet, who was really more of a punk than a Goth.

VON TEESE, DITA American pin-up starlet, fetish model and burlesque dancer (née Heather Renée Sweet, b. September 28, 1972), known to the general public for marrying (and divorcing) MARILYN MANSON, but beloved by lovers of glamour girls as this generation's BETTIE PAGE. The raven-haired beauty of the fake birthmark and red lips rocks the runway as well as the stripper pole and *Playboy* centerfold, often in the blackest, most decadent of dress, proving that you don't need to look like a SUICIDE GIRL to be a totally hot Goth.

VNV NATION English electronic music group founded in 1990 by singer Ronan Harris. The Gothiest thing about them is probably Harris's voice, with its icy detachment yet clean, mellifluous delivery. Initially, he paired that with straight-up EBM rhythms ripped from the Nitzer Ebb handbook, then evolved the project into happier, bouncier SYNTHPOP that has crossed over to the masses, at least in Europe. The soundtrack to CYBERGOTH life, much to the dismay of some old-school RIVETHEADS and DEATH ROCKERS. Essential tracks: "Further," "Chrome."

WEDNESDAY

WAVE-GOTIK-TREFFEN The world's biggest Goth festival, also known as WGT (pronounced Ve Ge Te) or simply Leipzig Fest, for the German city which has hosted it annually since 1992. Up to 200 bands of every conceivable gothy variety perform, while all-night dancing, all-day shopping (at what is probably the world's biggest Goth market) and other dark themed events (ABSINTHE brunch!) keep as many as 20,000 Goths busy for four days. Primarily attended by Germans (who are the most ÜBER of all, after all) and other Europeans, it does attract a significant number of North American Goths on pilgrimage. Amazingly, there is camping.

WAX TRAX! Chicago-based independent record label founded by Jim Nash and Dannie Flesher in 1978, originally as an import record shop that became the very influential home of INDUSTRIAL music in North America throughout the 1980s and early 1990s. It brought bands like Ministry, Front 242, My Life with the Thrill Kill Kult and KMFDM to the masses at a time when their heavy, often sleazy, electronic stomp was still underground, releasing such classic club tracks as 242's "Headhunter," Coil's "Tainted Love" and 1000 Homo DJ's "Supernaut," all while maintaining the retail shop as gathering place for bands and fans in the scene. While many of their acts jumped ship to major labels, Wax Trax! remained synonymous with the genre even after its bankruptcy and subsequent buy-out by TVT. The 1994 box set collection, *The Black Box*, compiles its greatest moments, of which there were many.

WEDNESDAY 1. Wednesday Addams, fictional child in the ADDAMS FAMILY comic/TV/film series whose PALE skin, pigtail braids and prim attire (not to mention, never smiling) have made her a Goth style icon. Played to wonderfully morose effect by Christina Ricci in the 1991 film. 2. Wednesday 13, American musician (né Joseph Poole, b. August 12, 1976) who took his stage name from the Addams girl and has fronted several HORROR PUNK bands, including Frankenstein Drag Queens from Planet 13 and Murderdolls, as well as releasing music as a solo artist. 3. Wednesday Mourning (née Jennifer Lee Smallwood, b. October 28, 1978), American self-identified Goth model, she of the waist-long black hair with perfect bangs, as seen in ads for KAMBRIEL. 4. Wednesday's Child, character in the English folk poem "Monday's Child," who is said to be full of woe and has obviously inspired quite a few woeful CHILDREN OF THE NIGHT.

WESTENRA, LUCY Fictional character in BRAM STOKER'S novel *DRACULA*; beautiful, sweet, gregarious best friend to Mina Harker, she is pursued by three suitors, plus one Count Dracula, who transforms her into his VAM-PIRE bride until she is staked by the hunter Van Helsing.

In the 1992 film version by Francis Ford Coppola, she is portrayed as a seductress by Sadie Frost.

WESTGATE GALLERY Website dedicated to the art, literature and culture of Death personified, run by noted necrophile author/artist Leilah Wendell. Originating as a small press in New York City in the 1970s, made famous as the Westgate Museum of Necromancy in New Orleans (a.k.a. "The House of Death") in the 1990s until its closure in 2005, Wendell's ongoing Azrael project now lives online where one can find out everything you ever needed to know about Death. (And get your Gothic Tarot cards read while you're at it.)

WEST MEMPHIS THREE Name given to Damien Echols, Jason Baldwin and Jessie Misskelley Jr., convicted of the murder of three eight-year-old boys in West Memphis, Arkansas, in 1993. The case has received considerable media attention and was the subject of two documentaries and the book *Devil's Knot*, in which supporters of the WM3 argue they were not given a fair trial. Many questions surround the actions of the police, who bungled evidence gathering and targeted Echols, the town misfit, because he was rumoured to be a Satanist. Various "Free the West Memphis Three" campaigns have been spearheaded by activists and artists, with benefit CDs, concerts, art shows and the like helping to fund their legal defense. Whether the three are guilty remains to be convincingly proven or disproven, but the fact that Echols sits on death row awaiting lethal injection primarily for being a strange, depressed kid who wore black, listened to Goth and metal music and read STEPHEN KING books should be of particular concern for anyone who cares that dressing like a FREAK should not be confused for a crime.

WESTWOOD, VIVIENNE British fashion designer (née Vivienne Isabel Swire, b. April 8, 1941) and grand dame of punk rock style. (Also, as of 1992, an actual Dame.) An art school drop-out and former teacher, she met future Sex Pistols manager Malcolm McLaren in 1965 and together they changed youth counter-culture forever with the opening of their clothing shop at 430 King's Road in London, known under various names over the years but none as infamous as SEX. Westwood combined her anglomania and love of classic tailoring with shocking style ripped from fetish wear to create the torn, tartan bondage look the world has come to associate with U.K. punks. Since then she has used everything from pirates, *Blade Runner* and Tudors for inspiration, and has been celebrated with an exhibit at the V & A Museum. Despite her associations with ADAM ANT, SIOUXSIE SIOUX and the like, there's nothing specifically Goth about her designs, with the wild colours and the political slogans. But for her outrageousness and extreme take on fashion, she is definitely a household name and much beloved.

WHITBY GOTHIC WEEKEND U.K. Goth festival held twice annually in the seaside town of Whitby, North Yorkshire (site of DRACULA's abbey, no coincidence), and sometimes referred to as WGW or simply Whitby. Founded in 1994, and still organized by Jo Hampshire, it boasts top-notch musical acts, DJs, shopping and some more unconventional events, such as a charity soccer match. A more TRAD GOTH experience than, say, WAVE-GOTIK-TREFFEN, its FAQ requests "taste and decency" when it comes to dress code, and participants do tend to sport elaborate VICTORIAN ballgowns. You might want to pack a PARASOL.

WICCA A Neopagan religion of modern witchcraft whose worshippers are often mistaken for Goths (or worse, Satanists), probably because of their fondness for pentagrams, CLOAKS, magic, candles and the like. Some Goths do indeed practice wicca and some wiccans are in fact Goth, but they are not interchangeable.

WIG Abbreviation for "What is Goth?," truly the philosophical question of our time.

WILLIAMS, ROZZ American musician (né Roger Alan Painter, 1963–1998) and Goth Martyr. In 1979, founded L.A. band CHRISTIAN DEATH, architect of California DEATH ROCK sound; the band's 1982 debut *Only Theatre of Pain* remains an underground classic. When he left the band and it continued under the leadership of member VALOR KAND, the battlelines were drawn: Goths are vehemently loyal to one singer or the other. Williams also recorded as performance art project Premature Ejaculation and straight-up Goth act Shadow Project (with wife Eva O.). None of these made him rich, but his legacy was eternally secured on April 1, 1998, when he hung himself in his Hollywood apartment. Ashes rest at Hollywood Forever Cemetery, Los Angeles.

WILSON, TONY The man who brought JOY DIVISION to the world (1950–2007). For a dramatized account of his life as a TV personality and co-founder of FACTORY RECORDS, see the film *24 Hour Party People*. Buried at Southern Cemetery, Cholton-cum-Hardy, Lancashire.

WINKLE PICKERS Shoe or boot with smooth, flat heel and an extremely, illogically pointed toe, sometimes referred to as "pikes." First seen on male rock 'n' rollers in the 1950s, developed into a stiletto heel for ladies in the 1960s and popularized by Goths of both genders in the 1980s with the addition of straps and buckles often featuring skulls or BATS. A TRAD GOTH wardrobe staple, despite the difficulty posed in climbing steps while wearing them. This term is primarily used in the U.K. *See also: Buckle boots*

WORLD GOTH DAY May 22, 2010, was declared a day for an organized celebration of Gothdom spearheaded by NIGHTBREED Radio in the U.K. Proposed activities included requesting Goth songs on the radio, hosting special events, baking evil cupcakes, etc. In 2011, added World Goth Day Awards, an online vote honouring best musicians, clubs, shops, and more.

WUMPSKATE Goth/INDUSTRIAL roller skating night, open to all ages and held monthly in Los Angeles. Yes, that says roller skating. Name is a pun on the GERMANY electro/industrial band :wumpscut:.

ZOMBIE

X-TRA-X German retailer of clothing and lifestyle accessories, since 1981. With four massive retail outlets throughout the country that stock Trad, Cyber, Lolita and other styles, host fashion shows, band autograph signings and more, plus their extensive online store, probably the biggest pusher of Gothic apparel in Europe. The original HOT TOPIC, ÜBER-sized.

YARBRO, CHELSEA QUINN American author of historical horror (b. September 15, 1942), best known as creator of the Count Saint-Germain series. Starting with 1978's *Hôtel Transylvania*, her more than two dozen novels re-imagine Saint-Germain (an actual shadowy occult figure from the past) as a VAMPIRE, then follow him around the world and through time, pitting him against everyone from the Incas to Ivan the Terrible. Along with ANNE RICE, Yarbro was one of the first to present vampires as heroic, sympathetic, romantic. Anyone can name-drop the Vampire LESTAT; for real GOTH POINTS, you read Yarbro.

YARNHEAD A person, usually CYBERGOTH, sporting a huge head of synthetic hair extensions, whether or not they are actually made from yarn. Derogatory.

ZILLO German magazine for Goth/electro/industrial/metal scene, launched in 1988 as a small zine (named for a club of the same name), now a glossy affair packed with the usual interviews and reviews with German and international acts and packaged with free sampler CDs. The comic strip "Dead," by Markus Zysk and Nicole Scheriau, has become a popular brand of merch. The magazine has also organized its own open air music festival most summers, heavy on the Goth bands.

ZOLA JESUS American singer (née Nika Roza Danilova, b. April 11, 1989), new on the scene but already leader of the newest wave of twenty-first century Goths — and not just because she's favourably compared to SIOUXSIE SIOUX and JOY DIVISION. A formally trained opera singer with killer vocal prowess, she composes atmospheric pop music with a sinister lyrical edge, enhanced by the use of stark, lo-fi, bedroom-quality production. So what if she's sometimes blonde? Her 2009 debut album, *The Spoils*, is a must-listen for those Goths still up for musical discovery.

ZOMBIE, ROB American singer and filmmaker (né Robert Bartlen Cummings, b. January 12, 1965), a rock 'n' roll star obsessed with horror movie monsters, who has given the world some groovy INDUSTRIAL metal riffs with his band White Zombie and on occasion some rather gothy homages. His biggest hit, "DRAGULA," is an ode to THE MUNSTERS; his "Living Dead Girl" is your best choice for a Goth stripper song out there, with a video based on the silent classic spookshow *The Cabinet of Dr. Caligari*. Zombie may not be Goth himself (no beard that untamed allowed!) but he's definitely your boogieman, *ye-eeeaaaaaaah*.

ZOMBIES Flesh-eating undead creatures of voodoo lore and modern horror movies who have crawled out of the earth and taken over from VAMPIRES as the creatures everyone loves most. Public zombie walks, and even zombie car washes, popped up all around the world in the 2000s, a place for people to paint the town fake blood red. Well, dare I say, no matter how much we love the idea of a ghoulish uprising, there is nothing Goth about dirty finger nails and bad table manners. Can we all go back to dressing up in CLOAKS and FANGS, please?

13 Goth Places to See Before You Die (or Afterwards)

13. CAMDEN MARKET (LONDON, U.K.)

Whether you're Trad Goth, Cybergoth or Goth Loli, best hold on tight to your credit cards at this alternative shopping mecca. You'll want to head straight to the zone called Stables Market, a former railway stables and horse hospital now lined with the most gothy of retailers ready to sell you the outfit of your dreams. Corsets at FairyGothmother. Poet shirts from Elizium. Neon alien-shaped dresses from Cyberdog. Elegant Victorian frocks from Sai Sai. And every kind of shoe or boot that ever stomped a dance floor. Sundays are the big day (the Electric Ballroom nightclub even opens an afternoon market), attracting tens of thousands, so even if you can't afford to buy much, there is plenty of eye candy. Hit it now before it's overrun with chain stores.

12. WHITBY GOTHIC WEEKEND (WHITBY, U.K.)

Now that you've purchased that long-dreamed-of, full-on Victorian ensemble at Camden Market, you need a place to wear it besides dark nightclubs with sticky floors. This Goth festival, located in a picturesque (read: touristy) town by the seaside five hours' drive north from London, offers live performances from top-name bands but also downright quaint daytime activities, from falconry displays to Gothic sandcastle building. A fine place for Steampunk role play too.

11. Bat Bridge (Austin, U.S.)

The city of Austin, Texas, is home to the largest urban bat colony in America. At sunset each night from March to November, as many as 1.5 million Mexican free-tailed bats come streaming out from under the Congress Avenue Bridge and fly off into the night in search of food. And if you stand on the bridge, or under it, or near it, you can marvel as wave after wave of our favourite nocturnal creatures swoop overhead. For free. You don't need to be a wildlife enthusiast or a cheapskate to know that's one of the coolest things ever.

10. Bone Church (Kutná Hora, Czech Republic)

So you like skulls and bones, do you? Might even have a real specimen in your home, purchased from some legitimate medical science supplier or stolen from a grave at night? The gothiest übergoth in all of Gothdom has nothing on the men who, in the

1800s, decorated the Sedlec Ossuary, a.k.a. the Bone Church. About an hour outside of Prague in the town of Kutná Hora, beneath a Gothic church and surrounded by a cemetery lies a tiny chapel adorned with the remains of up to 70,000 dead — their exhumed bones arranged to form chandeliers, coats of arms and other such décor. Sadly, they don't offer sleepovers.

9. ST. MARK'S PLACE (NEW YORK CITY, U.S.)

With all the Big Apple has to offer, why can I not resist coming to the same street in the East Village on every trip? Because this small strip (actually 8th Avenue between Third Avenue and Avenue A) is where you'll find the two-level shop Trash and Vaudeville, beacon of Goth and punk clothing. And while many of the other historic shops have long gone (Manic Panic, America's first punk boutique, for one), replaced by Japanese bubble tea shops and outdoor sunglass stalls, there remains a high freak factor, a concentration of alternative culture so rarely found, even in urban centres. And Yaffa Café still rocks the kitschy décor and vegetarian yums 24/7.

8. TORTURE GARDEN (VARIOUS)

The fetish party to end all fetish parties, headquartered in London where it hosts its famed monthly events, but also spreading its latex-sheathed wings to other cities such as Tokyo, New York, Toronto and beyond. The most creative outfits, the most outrageous performance art and the most diverse crowd of beautiful pervs you'll find anywhere. Halloween and New Year's Eve have never been so shiny.

7. HIGHGATE CEMETERY (LONDON, U.K.)

Any cemetery is worth a gander, a detour, a stroll through, of course. And one could argue that Paris's Père Lachaise would be the most Goth-worthy. But this graveyard in North London is the only one with its own vampire. If you believe the local lore, in the 1970s vampire ghosts were seen haunting this place. And even if you don't, it is the spot in Bram Stoker's *Dracula* where Lucy Westenra rises from the dead, plus it was used as a filming spot for the Hammer horror picture *Taste the Blood of Dracula*. With all this connection to bloodsuckers, visitors may wish to keep their necks covered up. Or not!

6. SLIMELIGHT (LONDON, U.K.)

Only Goths need apply at this famous warehouse nightclub. Seriously: it's a members-only club that at one time had an application form questionnaire testing your Goth knowledge. And since the 1980s, it's been spinning Goth, industrial and every subgenre derivation thereof every Saturday evening to Sunday morning. If you like to dance — or even just to stand

and argue about whether the Trad Goth floor DJ is playing Trad enough Goth music — you simply must pop by. Dress up and make friends with a member heading inside who can sign you in.

5. French Quarter (New Orleans, U.S.)

Well, Anne Rice and Trent Reznor don't live there anymore, so you can't stalk their mansions. And Hurricane Katrina did do some major damage to the city. But no Goth will be bored wandering the French Quarter of New Orleans. Rather, you will no doubt run out of time to take in all the ghost tours, cemetery walks, voodoo shops, absinthe bars and the like. In 2010, local DJs launched the Southern Gothic festival, the first of its kind in NOLA. Don't forget to tip the buskers; mimes gotta eat!

4. Bats Day at Disneyland (Anaheim, U.S.)

If you've always dreamed of going to Disneyland but the thought of spending the day in the hot California sun fills you with dread, why not go with people who will feel your pain — and not laugh at your parasol. At the annual Bats Day gathering, you'll join a few thousand Goths who take over the amusement park with glee. You might still have to wait in line for hours to enter the Haunted Mansion ride, but at least there will be someone to lend you some SPF 50 if you run out.

3. Transylvania (Romania)

Hungry for a taste of "the real Dracula"? Romania's tourism industry is banking you'll want to visit the country's historical sites connected to Vlad the Impaler, the Wallachian prince/warrior who allegedly inspired Bram Stoker's vampire count. Indeed there are castles aplenty throughout the region's Carpathian Mountains: the off-the-beaten track ruins of Poenari ("Dracula's Castle"), the medieval fortress Castle Bran ("Dracula's Castle") and the Snagov monastery ("Dracula's Tomb"). You can even rest your head at Dracula's Castle Hotel. For the most fang for your buck, sign up with Dracula Tours' Halloween weekend adventure.

2. Wave-Gotik-Treffen (Leipzig, Germany)

The world's greatest gathering of Goths of all stripes. A horde of pasty-faced girls and boys from all over Europe and the world descend upon this city two hours drive south of Berlin each summer to eat, drink, dance and be merry watching hundreds of band performances, shopping and creating, if only for a few days, a kind of All-Goth State. They quite literally terraform the place with velvet and PVC and clove smokes. Picture Mardi Gras and then in place of jazz and drunken girls flashing their boobs insert EBM and boys wearing fishnets and deathhawks. From the most über to Babybats and recovering Elder Goths in jeans, everyone is welcome.

1. Catacombs (Paris, France)

Above the stone portal entrance, a warning: *"Arrête, c'est ici l'empire de la mort."* ("Stop, here lies the empire of death.") What more of an invitation do you need? This subterranean ossuary beneath the streets of Paris is a dizzying maze of corridors pilled high with row upon row of skulls and bones. If being underground in a claustrophobic, dark space surrounded by human remains is on your bucket list, you won't find a better spot.

PUNK
NEW ROMANTICS
INDUSTRIAL
HORROR PUNK
Misfits
Balzac
The Independents
Calabrese
AFI
Murderdolls
PSYCHOBILLY
The Cramps
Demented Are Go
The Meteors
Mad Sin
Nekromantix
Horrorpops
The Damned
Siouxsie and the Banshees
The Gun Club
Nina Hagen Band
POST-PUNK
The Cure
The Fall
Joy Division
Gang of Four
Japan
Adam and the Ants
The Human League
Spandau Ballet
Culture Club
Yazoo
BATCAVE
Specimen
Sex Gang Children
Alien Sex Fiend
Cabaret Voltaire
Throbbing Gristle
Einstürzende Neubauten
Ministry
Skinny Puppy
NIN
Front Line Assembly
EBM
D.A.F.
Front 242
Leather Strip
Nitzer Ebb
Apoptygma Berzerk
:wumpscut:
VNV Nation
Combichrist
SYNTHPOP
Clan Of Xymox
Covenant
Switchblade Symphony
Project Pitchfork

THE CRÜXSHADOWS
THE BIRTHDAY MASSACRE

ECHO AND THE BUNNYMEN
KILLING JOKE
The BIRTHDAY PARTY
MARCH VIOLETS

ZOMBINA AND THE SKELETONES
Creepshow

INDUSTRIAL METAL

GODFLESH
KMFDM
YOUNG GODS
16 VOLT
marilyn manson
RAMMSTEIN
ORGY

ETHEREAL

COCTEAU TWINS
DCD DEAD CAN DANCE
THIS MORTAL COIL
BLACK TAPE FOR A BLUE GIRL
Bel Canto
Love Spirals Downward

DARKWAVE

LYCIA
Miranda Sex Garden
FAITH and the MUSE
Sopor Aeternus AND THE ENSEMBLE OF SHADOWS
DEINE LAKAIEN

DEATH ROCK

KOMMUNITY FK
UK DECAY
Christian Death
45 Grave
CINEMA STRANGE
Eat Your Make-up

GOTH ROCK

VIRGIN PRUNES
BAUHAUS
THE SISTERS OF MERCY
FIELDS OF THE NEPHILIM
the MISSION
nosferatu
London After Midnight

GOTHIC METAL

PARADISE LOST
TYPE O NEGATIVE
MY DYING BRIDE
CRADLE OF FILTH
HIM
LACUNACOIL
Nightwish

DARK CABARET

TIGER LILLIES
Strane Demone
JILL TRACY
THE DRESDEN DOLLS
EMILIE AUTUMN

Goth Band Tree

LYRICS PERMISSIONS

BLACK PLANET

Words and music by Andrew Eldritch and Wayne Hussey
Copyright © 1985 ELDRITCH BOULEVARD LTD.
and UNIVERSAL MUSIC PUBLISHING MGB LTD.
All rights for ELDRITCH BOULEVARD LTD. in the United
States and Canada controlled and administered by UNIVERSAL
– POLYGRAM INTERNATIONAL PUBLISHING, INC.
All rights for UNIVERSAL MUSIC PUBLISHING MGB LTD.
in the United States and Canada controlled and administered
by UNIVERSAL MUSIC – MGB SONGS
All rights reserved. Used by permission.
Reprinted by permission of Hal Leonard Corporation

GOTH GIRLS IN THE CALIFORNIA SUN

Words and music by David Haskins
Copyright © 2002 Urbane Music
All rights reserved. Used by permission.
Reprinted by permission of David Haskins

ACKNOWLEDGEMENTS

This book would not have been possible without the support of many colleagues and friends, and the writing on Goth that came before it.

Firstly, to the team at ECW Press, particularly Michael Holmes for saying yes and Crissy Boylan for making it better with her keen eye. And to Gary Pullin for his incredibly wicked illustrations. It's an honour to work with you all.

Of the many excellence reference tomes on Gothic music and culture already penned, I drew inspiration and information from *Dark Entries: Bauhaus and Beyond* by Ian Shirley, *The Dark Reign of Gothic Rock: In the Reptile House with The Sisters of Mercy, Bauhaus and The Cure* by Dave Thompson, *Rip it Up and Start Again: Postpunk 1978–1984* by Simon Reynolds, *Goth Chic: A Connoisseur's Guide to Dark Culture* by Gavin Baddeley and *The Goth Bible* by Nancy Kilpatrick, as well as the archives of alt.gothic, goth.net, waningmoon.org and *Propaganda*, *Ghastly*, *Permission*, *Gothic Beauty*, *NME*, *Sounds* and *Melody Maker* magazines.

I would not have been in the position to write this book without being Goth in the first place, so thanks to the DJs who changed the soundtrack of my life: The Brother, Denise Benson, Dani "Alternative Bedtime Hour" Elwell, DJ Iain, TK Kelly, Mitch "Beyond the Gates of Hell" Krol, DJ Lazarus, Lord Pale, Ivan Palmer, Paul and John from Empire Mondays, Mr. Pete, Scary Lady Sarah, Stephen Scott, DJ Shannon and Chris Sheppard. And most especially the dearly missed Martin Streek, who was not Goth but knew that every day could be Halloween but Halloween was the best day of all.

Of equal importance in my Gothucation were the many cut 'n' pasted photocopied zines that filled my mailbox and captured my imagination throughout the 1990s. *Theatre of the Night*, *Nyx Obscura*, *Among the Ruins*, *Thistle* and the rest: R.I.P.

For valuable assistance during the process of getting this out of my head and onto the published page: Gillian Holmes, Stacey Mitsopulos and Tony Burgess, my Goth reading team of Stephanie "50footqueenie" Quinlan, Laura "Morbid Outlook" McCutchan and Sharon "Not a Goth" Hughes, plus the many Goths around the planet I hassled.

Finally, I am lucky to have people in my life who've long supported me and my writing. Much gratitude to my girlfriends Sharon, Carol, Andrea, Karen and Ankixa, who I can always count on for adventures and who would never try to stop me from riding a bike in a velvet cloak. To the Royal Sarcophagus Society, because Art Saves. To the truly incredible Deane, who always knew I had it in me and never let me forget it and for being the boy who would let me paint his nails black. To my black cat, Nisha, for the incessant hugs. And to my mother, Marie, who may not be much of a reader but knew enough to instill in me a love of language early on and who always stuck up for me and my wacky Goth hairdos. I love you all.

LIISA LADOUCEUR is a music and unpopular culture journalist, a poet, and a Goth. A former Goth zine publisher, she has examined the subculture for various newspapers and magazines and been called upon as a recognized expert on radio and television including MuchMusic, Newsworld, CTV and TVO. Her arts reporting has been published in *Eye Weekly*, *National Post*, *THIS Magazine*, *BUST* and *Alternative Press* and she has appeared regularly on MuchMoreMusic and CBC Radio. She is currently known as the Blood Spattered Guide music columnist for *Rue Morgue*, the world's leading publication for horror in art and culture. Liisa lives in Toronto, Ontario, and still owns a hair crimper.